A Gift of Words

by

John (Jack) Stevens

i

DEDICATION

To the grandchildren
Unfortunately I cannot afford to leave each of you with a large inheritance when I pass on. However in reading our family story I hope you all will gain an appreciation of the struggles your forefathers endured during their lives. Also I trust that you will find a few words of wisdom in our family history to assist you in your own journey through life.
God Bless
Grandpa Jack Stevens

ACKNOWLEGEMENTS

This book would not have been possible without the help of many people. I want to particularly thank all my cousins who so willingly shared special memories of their summer vacations on the Stevens farm many years ago.

In addition a debt of gratitude goes out to cousins Andy and Myra Morin, Fee and Anne Otterson, Ken and Larry McGillis and Ann Littleton for their help. The photos and other materials you so willingly provided me with helped immeasurably in bringing the early Stevens and Franz family history alive.

Special thanks go out to my editor and publisher Charles Goulet. Charles is an accomplished author who writes historical novels based on French Canadian History. He also has his own publishing company Chronicler Publishing.

I also want to thank my grandson Cameron LaRocque for his many hours of dedicated assistance. Without his excellent computer skills I would have been totally lost in putting this book together. Most of all without Joyce's encouragement and patience this project would not have been possible.

A GIFT OF WORDS
By John "Jack" Stevens

INTRODUCTION

When one starts the difficult task of attempting to write a meaningful account of our ancestors and highlights of our own family, the question comes to mind "Why record family history?"

The saying that life is lived forward but understood backward rings true as we get older. We all have stages in our lives from the exuberance of our youth to the tranquility of old age (God willing). I think it is important that we attempt to discover our roots and be aware of the struggles and triumphs of our ancestors.

A family genealogy chart can provide us with vital information on our ancestors. These facts however valuable do not give us a true picture into how or where our forefathers lived out their lives.

The common thread of our Franz and Stevens ancestors that I admire was their spirit of adventure. Their willingness to look beyond the horizon in their later years was admirable.

To quote imminent Western Canadian Izzy Asper, founder of Can West Global Television in discussing his own Russian roots he said, "Everybody is a product of geography and timing." The decision by Izzy's musician father to emigrate to Minnedosa, Manitoba is responsible for his family not ending up as cinders in Hitler's gas chambers.

As our family story unfolds we will see how geography and timing were perhaps factors in great grandfather Jacob Franz's final journey of discovery to Western Canada in 1899. Why he chose the yet to be formed province of Alberta and more specifically the Edmonton area as his final destination we will never know.

Unfortunately my grandparents, John and Mary Stevens, left little written record of their formative years in South Dakota. They did however leave us a legacy of early family photos, newspaper clippings and letters. These were of great assistance in writing a meaningful account of their early years.

My parents John and Nora Stevens also left us no formal biographies of their lives. Mom did however assist in helping to compile a local history book. Aunt Ellen McGillis, Aunt Margaret Fitzgerald and mom were part of a committee that was responsible for seeing this project through to its completion. Their efforts plus the work of the many others left us with an excellent local history book aptly named, The Wheels of Time.

I like the following quote by Barb Glenn Editor of the Western Producer Farm Paper. In an editorial she wrote discussing the importance of recording family history, she said the following: "How can we gauge how far we've come if that distance isn't measured by history? How can we take pride in our own roots without knowing their origins? It comes down to this, recognizing the past shows us the limitless potential of the future."

CHAPTER ONE

In an effort to escape the oppression of their English Masters and I presume as a result of the potato famine in Ireland in the 1840s both my paternal great grandmother's families, the O'Donnell's and the Donovan's, left Ireland in search of a better life in the U. S.

A courageous decision made by my paternal great grandfather Jacob Franz to leave Germany to seek opportunities in a far away land resulted in him arriving in the U. S. some time before 1861. Although we have no official documentation we think great great grandfather Abraham Stevens put down roots shortly before 1800 in the United States.

CHAPTER TWO

The first record we have of our branch of the Stevens family in North America was the marriage of great great grandfather Abraham Stevens to Lucy Whittemore on November third 1813, at the Trinity Episcopal Church in Utica, New York. His profession was listed as a gunsmith, which I presume was an excellent occupation in those early frontier days.

According to cousin Laverle Stevens of Sioux Falls, South Dakota, Abraham was an accomplished violinist having played with one of the symphony orchestras in London, England. We would have to give some credence to this story in that great grandfather John Stevens was also an accomplished musician. The musical genes were also passed down to my grandfather John Stevens and also his younger brother Henry who played in local bands in South Dakota.

Great grandfather John Stevens was born on May 15th, 1819 at Utica, New York. Unfortunately we have no information on how many children were in the Abraham and Lucy Stevens family. We also have no record on the date of great grandfather's first marriage or the date of his wife's passing. There were two children from his first marriage Lucy and George who are mentioned as performing musical selections in his early panorama presentations.

CHAPTER THREE

Great grandfather John Stevens like many of his generation joined the great westward trek of people seeking to explore America's undeveloped western frontier.

He first went to Illinois and from there to Wisconsin. In 1853 he traveled to the present site of Rochester, Minnesota, which at the time was a piece of raw unbroken prairie soil. He then proceeded to build a home at this yet unnamed frontier location.

In 1854 a party of U. S. government surveyors set stakes through what is now Olmsted County, Minnesota. George Head was the first permanent settler in the new town of Rochester. He named it Rochester for the reason the small falls nearby reminded him of the small water falls back home at Rochester, New York. By coincidence the main street of the new town Rochester passed directly by great grandfather's newly built house.

We would have to assume that accommodations were at a premium in this new frontier community. In 1856 great grandfather never one to miss an opportunity converted his home to a hotel that he called The Stevens House the first hotel to be built in Rochester. A few years later he sold the hotel however for many years after it was still known as the Stevens House.

His next venture was sign painting, doing some prior to selling his hotel. He was described as a skilled sign painter. One of his earlier works was painting the emblem on the float that carried the members of Rochester's traveling band. As we indicated earlier he had a talent for music and played in the local Rochester band. In the future great grandfather would take his sign painting to the next level painting panoramas. However in 1859 he had more important things on his mind.

CHAPTER FOUR

In March of 1859 great grandfather married an Irish Catholic girl named Ann Donovan at La Crosse, Wisconsin. Before marrying great grandmother he became a convert to the Catholic faith. Great grandfather was forty years old and great grandmother was twenty-three when they were married.

Great grandmother was born on May 1st, 1836 in Cork County, Ireland.

CHAPTER FIVE

The gradual encroachment of white settlers into the traditional land of the Native American Indians was one of the watershed events of the mid nineteenth century in the Western United States. In August of 1862 some young Sioux braves attacked a remote white settlement in an area of Minnesota called Shelek Lake. The most dramatic part of the story was how a young boy named Merton Eastlick managed to carry his baby brother to safety. This involved a journey of sixty miles over a period of four days. Three other brothers and their father had lost their lives in the attack. The mother of the family was wounded, but miraculously survived.

The Lake Shelek uprising must of caught great grandfather's imagination. He correctly assumed that painting and exhibiting a Panorama of the uprising would have a dramatic appeal and news value in the frontier settlements. He therefore began work on painting his first panorama.

They could be described as primitive newsreels or movies in that they showed the major events of the day in the form of painted scenes on long rolls of canvass. Unknown to great grandfather at the time was that painting and exhibiting panoramas would become the main focus of most his remaining years.

His Sioux War Panorama consisted of thirty-six individual oil paintings on a continuous piece of canvass approximately two hundred and twenty feet long and seven feet in height. The individual scenes were seven feet high and eight feet wide. Just doing one scene would take many hours of paintings. How he managed to paint and assemble these large rolls of painted scenes in I am assuming not too spacious Art Studio is a feat in itself.

Prior to showing the panorama he set up a mechanical picture screen that was a wooden frame about eight feet wide and seven feet high. It consisted of two horizontal rollers, one at the top and one at the bottom. Gears and a hand crank controlled their rotation. Rolled up on the bottom roller and ready to roll up around the top roller was the panorama. Two oil lamps under the frame added to the authenticity of the scenes being depicted when shown at night. Great grandfather would act as the narrator standing on one side with the person who turned the crank standing on the opposite side who would slowly unroll the panorama upward.

CHAPTER SIX

While great grandfather was painting his Sioux War Panorama he had the occasion to travel to St. Charles, Minnesota on a stagecoach. On the way there one of the other passengers on the stage was a survivor of the Lake Shelek massacre, a Mrs. Lamina Eastlick.

As we alluded to earlier her husband was killed in the uprising, plus three of her children. In his conversations with Mrs. Eastlick great grandfather indicated that he had about four weeks left to complete his Sioux War panorama as he called it. He offered to donate the proceeds of his first panorama showing scheduled for Winona, Minnesota to Mrs. Eastlick. She was however anxious to talk to the other survivors of the uprising and declined great grandfather's generous offer.

Several weeks later Mrs. Eastlick went back to Rochester to see as she described, "My artist friend Mr. Stevens". Great grandfather had not quite finished his panorama however he graciously agreed to show his yet uncompleted panorama. He donated the proceeds of twelve dollars to Mrs. Eastlick. She is quoted as saying of great grandfather, "He is a man of great generosity".

Later Mrs. Eastlick and her two surviving children stopped at Rochester on their way to St. Charles, Minnesota. She described herself as being very tired no doubt from the traumatic experience of losing her husband and sons. She also had no visible means of support for her young family and herself. Early next morning she went to my great grandparent's home planning to travel on to St. Charles that day however in her own word she said, "His kind hearted wife urged me to stay with them and rest myself till the next day" which she did.

They also invited her oldest son Merton to stay with them for several months, which she accepted. Two months later great grandfather brought him back to Mrs. Eastlick sister's home in Wisconsin where she was staying. She quotes "Two months afterward he brought him to me he was much attached to his benefactor and on the day that Mr. Stevens left him to go farther east he wept for nearly an hour".

CHAPTER SEVEN

Great grandfather finished painting his first Sioux War Panorama in early 1863. As there were no Movie Theaters in those early days we would have to assume that he showed his panorama wherever he could find a gathering place large enough to accommodate his primitive screen and an audience.

In 1864 my great grandparents moved back to La Crosse, Wisconsin where they had been married just five years earlier. La Crosse is a very scenic city on the St. Croix River located about sixty miles straight east of Rochester, Minnesota. It is possible that great grandmother had family there or great grandfather may have thought the opportunities for showing and promoting his panorama would be better at La Crosse.

Great grandfather not being quite satisfied with his original panorama painting began working on a new panorama. In 1865 the La Crosse Democrat reported that he was working on a more elaborate version of his original panorama. In the fall of 1865 he entered some of his newly painted scenes in the La Crosse County Fair and won several awards.

CHAPTER EIGHT

On December 5th, 1867 Grandfather John Stevens was born at La Crosse, Wisconsin the first born of my great grandfather's second family. I am sure great grandfather did not realize the practice of using the name John for the first boy born in the succeeding Stevens family would continue for the next six generations. It was however very fragile name succession considering three of the next five generations had only one boy in their respective families.

The first John was great grandfather John Stevens, then my grandfather John D. Stevens, followed by my dad John I. Stevens. Then myself John D. Stevens, continuing with (Uncle John) John M. Stevens and the last John, John Jordan Stevens.

1867 also officially marked the birth of Canada as a country. The other big news item of that year was the United States purchase of Alaska for seven million two hundred thousand dollars from Russia. Had this purchase not occurred world and Canadian history might have evolved in a very different manner.

CHAPTER NINE

In February of 1868 great grandfather presented his newly painted panorama at La Crosse before a large audience. A month later on the evening of March 5th it was presently with much fan fare at the Opera House in St. Paul Minnesota. Prior to the showing Munger Bros music store sold tickets for fifty cents with reserve seats priced at seventy-five cents. Below is an old copy of the poster advertising great grandfather's panorama presentation of March 5th at the St. Paul Opera House. We note from reading the poster that he was pretty dramatic in describing his upcoming presentation.

OPERA HOUSE.

Thursday Evening, March 5th.

The Most Extraordinary Exhibition in the World!

STEVENS'
GREAT
TABLEAU PAINTINGS
REPRESENTING THE
INDIAN MASSACRE
IN MINNESOTA IN 1862.

THE GREAT MORAL EXHIBITION
OF THE AGE!

This is the most thrilling Exhibition ever offered to the public. It was commenced in 1862, and has been in steady progress until the present time, requiring a vast amount of labor. It was executed by that Celebrated Artist, JOHN STEVENS, who has visited the different localities, and taken many of the Sketches on the spot.

CAPT. C. E. SENCERBOX
Will delineate the different scenes.

Commencing with a Life-Like View of the North End of

LAKE SHETEK
Opening of the Outbreak of Aug. 20, 1862.

A View of the residence of Mr. Myers—Indians Destroying his Grain, &c.
A View of the house of Mr. Hurd—Shooting of Mr. Voight—Flight of Mrs. Hurd and Children, &c.
Interior View of Mr. Hurd's Residence—Indians Destroying its contents.

House of Mr. Cook, a Beautiful Landscape Scene.
Murder of Mr. Cook and capture of his Wife—Thrilling narrative of her sufferings.

CHARLES HATCH Bringing NEWS OF THE OUTBREAK to the Settlers!
Flight of the Eastlick Family and other Settlers in a wagon—Men armed and covering their retreat, Indians mounted and in pursuit—Women abandon the wagon—Battle with the Indians—Slaughter of nearly all the male portion of the Settlers—Capture of the Women—Old Women and Children Killed.

FLIGHT OF THE NOBLE BOY, MURTON EASTLICK!
With his Infant Brother, 18 months old, in his arms, whom he carries 52 miles to a place of safety.

ESCAPE OF MRS. EASTLICK!
And a Graphic Description of her Sufferings, etc.

WAR DANCE, AT NIGHT.
Indians showing in pantomime the struggles and contortions of their victims of the day before.

PORTRAITS
Of LITTLE HILL, Winnebago Chief. ROSE ROSS, one of the principal Actors in the great Massacre, the Indian that captured Mrs. Cook. MRS. COOK in her Indian Costume. OTHER DAY, a friendly Chief that saved 62 Whites. RED IRON, friendly Sioux, that delivered the captives to Gen. Sibley at Camp Release. NES-QUA-SH and WA-KE-TIE, or FLYING SKY. Also Portraits of nearly every Indian Chief that was engaged in the Massacre.

FULL LENGTH PORTRAIT OF GENERAL SIBLEY.

Grand and Imposing Spectacle, A Bird's-Eye View of NEW-ULM!

VIEW OF THE FALLS OF ST. ANTHONY.

THRILLING SCENES!

Killing of Captain Dodd, in the Attack on New Ulm. Indian Attack on a party engaged in threshing near St. Peter—Massacre of the men and capturing horses. Killing of Mrs. Smith and daughter by Chief Knitting Runner. Murder of 18 Women and Children in a wagon, by CUT NOSE. A FULL LENGTH PORTRAIT of this Demon.

CHASKA,	OLD BETS.
The Murderer of George Gleason, and Captured of the Wakefield Family.	A great favorite with both Whites and Indians.

View of Camp Release. Surrender of the Female Captives to Gen. Sibley by Red Iron.
Hanging of 38 Indians at Mankato. View of a portion of the City of Mankato.

Tickets 50 cts. Reserved Seats 25 cts. extra.
For sale at Munger Bros. Music Store, on Thursday morning, at 8 o'clock.
Doors open in the Evening at 7 o'clock. To commence at 8 o'clock precisely.

7

Perhaps buoyed with his recent successful showing in St. Paul, Minnesota my great grandparents moved back to Rochester, Minnesota. However the most interesting aspect of their move was that great grandfather was working on yet another new and improved panorama. This panorama was to be a total new style with transparent colors being used. The lights would now be placed behind the panorama scenes rather than in front of them when showing it to the public.

The Rochester Post described them as "Diaphanous Painting" defined as method newly invented by the Rochester painter. Great grandfather completed his new panorama in October 29th, 1870 with the first showing in Rochester on November 5th of that year. The paper reported that the panorama was shown before a "good audience" with Stevens himself reading the "beautiful oratorical explanations" that went with the scenes.

CHAPTER TEN

Our family is fortunate to have copies of some old letters of great grandfather John Stevens. Great grandfather wrote the following letters to great grandmother some time during 1868. They reflected what life on the road was like in 1868 with his traveling panorama. Exerts of the letters from long ago appear below.

"I just got back from Lebanon, from a trip around Cincinnati, we showed in the city one night and made a little. But it is risky business to show in such large cities as it costs five hundred to advertise and it is all chance whether you make or lose. I rise at five o'clock in the morning and then it is pack up the panorama and git off to the next place. I just tell you that my paintings still gits the name of being the finest that has been exhibited in this country"

The Lebanon great grandfather is referring to is in the State of Indiana and Cincinnati is in Ohio. He had traveled many miles east from Minnesota. He was perhaps attempting to reach areas where the people were not even aware of the Shelek uprising in Minnesota. Five hundred dollars was a huge sum of money to pay for advertising in those early days. No wonder great grandfather focused on smaller rural towns for his panorama showings.

Exerts from another letter to great grandmother mention their plans to buy some land, "My dear wife keep up good cheer. I hope our better days are coming, if I can make enough to buy a farm, we will be all right"

CHAPTER ELEVEN

No doubt great grandmother Ann Donovan had rural roots. The majority of the Irish Catholics were very poor. At the outbreak of the potato famine in 1845 many families lived on half-acre plots of land owned by absentee English Landlords. They referred to as tenant farmers. Although their existence was sparse they still had a love for the land. Many of the Irish when coming to the U. S. carried the dream with them of being masters of their own destiny. I am sure great grandmother was partly instrumental in my great grandparent's dreams of eventually having a piece of land to call their own.

CHAPTER TWELVE

In January of 1873 great grandfather hired Merton Eastlick who he had befriended years earlier as a lecturer and manager with his winter panorama tour. He also agreed to give Merton and his family half the proceeds of their winter tour. This was a very kind gesture by great grandfather to assist a family that had suffered so much.

The Rochester Post reported that the panorama was stored in a "traveling rig" which according to the Post was "like the panorama itself, something very unique". It was described as, "A long covered sleigh" with "sides of transparent canvass on which are painted striking advertisements of the show". These were "covered up when on the road but exhibited on entering towns" where the panorama was to be displayed. To attract attention in the evening the sleigh was "brilliantly lit from inside". The exhibitors kept snug and warm by a stove inside the sleigh and were able to "furnish the people with music" as they drove through the streets.

In October of 1873 great grandfather launched another panorama tour opening in Spring Valley, Wisconsin. It took him to many remote towns and villages in Wisconsin and Iowa. The winter tour of 1873-74 was perhaps the most successful of all his winter tours. In March of 1874 a Rochester paper reported that he was "well satisfied with his winter's campaign".

CHAPTER THIRTEEN

Shown below is a framed copy of an old hand bill of great grandfather's advertising an upcoming panorama presentation. It is courtesy of Cousin Anne Otterson having been among her mother's keepsakes that she passed on to me. We now have it displayed with other old family keepsakes in our recreation room downstairs.

Prof. STEVENS

will give a

LECTURE

on the

Indian Massacre in Minnesota

in 1862, closing with the execution of

38 Indians at Mankato,

and on Gen.

CUSTER'S EXPEDITION

in the Black Hills, and on his last Battles, with

Panorama Oil Paintings

To represent the same, in forty-nine scenes. Passing an opening 7 by 9 feet and delineated by Prof. Stevens, who was an eye witness to some of the scenes, commencing with a view of the north end of Lake Sheteck, where the Indians commenced to kill the Whites.

BEST'S BLOCK, BRIDGE SQ.

Monday & Tuesday Eve's Feb. 17 & 18.

Has followed painting 40 years. Prof. Stevens took the

FIRST PREMIUM

ON

Portrait Painting at the State Fair at St. Paul.

All lovers of fine art should not fail to see these Paintings, they are highly spoken of by the press. Life-like portraits of all the leading chiefs in the Massacre.

Admission 10 and 20 cts.

Best's Block, Bridge Square.

Doors open at 7. Commencing at 7:30.

Davison & Hall, Print.

Also among the items that we have of Great grandfathers is a section of another old hand bill promoting a Panorama of the Black Hills. I have no idea what the dancing skeleton involved however it made a good headline.

11

The balloon ascension would also have been a huge event of that era. By reading what is left of the handbill we can see that he employed very creative advertising in promoting his upcoming panorama presentations.

Copy of Old Bill Advertising Panorama

CHAPTER FOURTEEN

In November of 1874 great grandfather sold his latest panorama painting for as the Rochester Post reported "the handsome sum of two thousand dollars" to a buyer in Wisconsin.

Great grandfather's sale may have been motivated by a serious recession or panic as they called it in those days that began in the U. S. in 1873. A lot of railroad lines had been built on speculation with the resulting lines being very unprofitable. Joy Cooke and Company a large New York bank was heavily indebted to the eighty-nine railroad companies. When the railroads defaulted on their loans the bank also became insolvent. The recession lasted for three years with three million people being put out of work. Ironically one hundred and twenty three years later over expansion in the U. S. housing market created an even greater calamity. I guess the lesson here is that excessive speculation in any industry often has dire results.

With some of the proceeds from the sale of the panorama I assume great grandfather purchased an eighty-acre farm in 1875. It was located about twenty miles west of Rochester at Dodge Center, Minnesota. The purchase price was five hundred dollars and which included a mortgage of two hundred dollars at 12% per annum. No cheap money in those early days.

Also at some point great grandfather had also acquired three hundred and twenty acres of homestead land about two hundred seventy five miles west of Dodge Center, located in McCook County, near Canistota, South Dakota.

CHAPTER FIFTEEN

On August 8th, 1879 great grandfather passed away at home on his Minnesota farm at sixty years of age as the result of contacting cholera. My grandfather John Stevens at twelve years old became man of the house. We would have to assume this ended any of grandfather's previous carefree childhood days.

The obituary below was in the Rochester Post on Friday August 15th, 1879 announcing great grandfather's passing. We are indebted to the History Center of Olmstead County Rochester, Minnesota for sending us this obituary.

Obituary—Stevens.

Mr. John Stevens, well known throughout the state, and one of the earliest settlers of this county, died at his home, five miles south of Dodge Center, on Sunday morning last, at the age of sixty years. Mr. Stevens was taken ill on the 2d of August when he appeared to be in his usual good health, and after an illness of only eight days, he died.

Mr. Stevens was born in Utica, New York, on the 15th of May, 1819. At an early day he emigrated to Illinois, and from there to Wisconsin. In 1853 he came to this place, which was at that time nothing but a vast tract of unbroken land. After remaining here a month or two he returned to Iron Ridge, Wisconsin, where he purchased a drove of horses, and returned here the following year and located.

Mr. Stevens is probably as well known as any of the early settlers of Rochester. In 1856 he built, and was for a few years proprietor of the Stevens House, on Main street, and in 1858 sold it to Mr. Fleck. The Stevens House stood on the ground now covered by the Pierce House, and was burned down in March, 1877.

After leaving the hotel, Mr. Stevens followed his profession as house and sign painter, and in later years gained considerable notoriety as a panoramic artist. His panoramas of the Minnesota Indian Massacre in 1862, the Modoc War, and of the Chicago Fire, are well known throughout this state, Wisconsin and Iowa.

A few years ago Mr. Stevens disposed of his panoramas, and removed to his farm near Dodge Center, where with assistance, he has conducted his farm, and devoted most of his time to portrait painting. He also owned a farm of three hundred and twenty acres in McCook county, Dakota, that is well under cultivation, and provided with suitable dwellings, barns, etc. He returned from his farm in Dakota the latter part of July, and he had only been at home eleven days when he was prostrated with a severe attack of cholera morbus from which he never recovered.

His remains were brought to this city on Monday, and funeral services were held at St. John's Church.

Great Grandfather John Stevens in his later years, photo courtesy of Laverle Stevens, Sioux Falls, South Dakota

CHAPTER SIXTEEN

The information in the above obituary helped solve the puzzling references by grandfather's sister Kate of great grandfather painting scenes of Indians camped by the Vermillion River near Canistota, South Dakota. In addition Aunt Mae also mentioned grandfather recalling his mother had planted a tree on land close to their farm. The records at the McCook County Register of deeds confirm a Homestead was originally registered in the name of great grandfather John Stevens. It was located about four miles northwest of the farm the Franz family would eventually purchase in the same area.

Upon great grandfather's passing the land was transferred to his daughter Lucy Stevens who was the administrator of his Estate. In February of 1890 Lucy Quick claimed the land to grandfather. It was put up for auction and grandfather bought the land for one thousand dollars cash. The proceeds I assume were shared with his siblings.

We were unable to locate great grandfather headstone in the beautiful old Calvary Cemetery Rochester, Minnesota on our visit there in 2002. An old family hand written note indicates that great grandfather's plot location to be 274 and 275 Block 2. We would have to assume by the two numbers that one plot was reserved for great grandmother on her passing. However events would intervene making that not possible. Unfortunately when we called at cemetery office they indicated that their records were incomplete for 1879 the year of grandfather's death. There is a distinct possibility that we could face the same scenario as with great grandmother Anne's gravesite in that no permanent grave marker was used.

Grandfather's sister Kate had always maintained that her father was buried in Rochester. Although Kate was only five years old at the time of her father's passing it no doubt made a lasting impression on her. Among the old newspaper clippings belonging to our family was one sent to grandma Stevens in 1951. It was taken from an article in the Rochester Post Bulletin dated Wednesday January 31st, 1951. The headline read, John Stevens Early Artist Buried here. This was the same paper the great grandfather's obituary notice had appeared in some sixty-two years earlier.

The paper based their information on correspondence that the Calvary Cemetery had received from grandfather's sister Kate. In her letter she confirmed that great grandfather was indeed laid to rest in the Calvary Cemetery at Rochester. His obituary in the Rochester Post Bulletin indicated that his services were held at St. John's church in Rochester with logical conclusion being he was also laid to rest in the local Calvary Cemetery.

CHAPTER SEVENTEEN

Another interesting bit of information included in his obituary notice indicated that great grandfather had at some point painted a panorama of the Modoc Indian Massacre of 1873 and the huge Chicago Fire of 1871.

16

With my strong Irish heritage I was curious on following up on Mrs. O'Leary often being referred to as the individual responsible for the huge Chicago Fire of 1871. On a recent visit to the St. Albert library I noticed a new huge very well written book entitled Chicago a Biography by Dominic A. Pacyga who teaches in the Department of Humanities, History, and Social Sciences at Columbia College Chicago.

According to Professor Pacyga's research the fire originated in the poor west side working class section of Chicago. The actual site where the fire started was in the barn of Catherine O'Leary who ran a small milk business. Apparently a load of hay had been just delivered to Mrs. O'Leary prior to the start of the devastating Chicago fire. Popular folklore at the time assumed that Mrs. O'Leary's cow had kicked over a lantern during the evening milking. However there was no official documentation of this being the actual cause of the fire. By some miracle the O'Leary home was not destroyed in the fire. Two Catholic churches on the west side of Chicago somehow managed to survive the fire also. Catholics were widely hated at the time of the fire especially Irish Catholics. This of course caused rumors of a possible Romanist conspiracy. In 1871 the people of Chicago had a hard time accepting that poor Mrs. O'Leary had not started this great conflagration intentionally. Ironically the Irish who made up a large segment of Chicago's west side poor working class suffered greatly as a result of the fire.

To put into perspective the enormity of this great fire it managed to destroy 17,450 buildings many of them who were supposedly fireproof. Included in the loss were The Chicago Court House, The Post Office and Railroad Station. The property damage as result of the fire approached two hundred million dollars a huge amount for that time period. Thirty thousand people were given free railroad passes to leave Chicago to help alleviate the shortage of available shelter as a result of the fire.

CHAPTER EIGHTEEN

When we examine great grandfather's life there are just twenty-three years from which any meaningful information is available. During these years being a widower with two children he married great grandmother and started a second family. He also established his first business venture The Stevens House the first Hotel in Rochester. We would have to assume with great grandfather's talent for meeting and working with people he would have been very successful as an Hotelier.

However he definitely took the road less traveled and followed his passion for painting and showing panoramas as his life's work. Painting thirty six large different scenes on a two hundred and twenty foot canvass was in itself a huge undertaking. Great grandfather was never quite satisfied with his work. He was successful in producing improved versions of his original panorama paintings on more than one occasion.

The main subject of his panoramas focused on the Sioux Indian Wars. Also included were scenes from the Black Hills and The Yellow Stone Country with depictions of many other current news events. He witnessed huge American watershed events during his lifetime two of which were the Civil war and the assassination of Abraham Lincoln. His early panoramas were the newsreels and travelogues of the nineteenth century.

He showed a lot of compassion for the Eastlick family in helping them overcome their tragic loss of family members. In hiring Henry Horton a Negro to travel and perform with his panorama he showed respect for a visible minority long before it was politically correct to do so. It is interesting that the Horton family had one of his original panoramas that is now in the Minnesota History Center in St. Paul. One has to wonder if he gave them this panorama as a gift.

Great grandfather seemed to have a flare for promotion as the advertising on the old hand bills we have of his indicate. To have your work preserved and discussed long after your life is over is a definite mark of accomplishment. The panorama's he painted depicting the struggles of the early settlers in the American mid west have now become an important part of American frontier history. However the ultimate tribute any one can ever hope to have said about them was written in a simple short sentence at the conclusion of another obituary in the Rochester Record and Union newspaper Friday, August 15th 1879. "He was an honest man and was respected by all who knew him".

CHAPTER NINETEEN

Before we finish this section on great grandfather's life I would like to include how the later life of two of my great grandparent's friends evolved Mrs. Eastlick and her son Merton. Merton was very attached to great grandfather as a young child and later was a lecturer and manager of his 1873 winter panorama tour. Mrs. Eastlick story contains some happiness and a lot of heartbreak.

Thinking the reader of this narrative would be pleased to know of my whereabouts and how I have been getting along these many years, I will give a short sketch.

After visiting my relatives in Wisconsin I went to Ohio where my mother and father lived. They received me and mine with joy and many tears. I remained in Ohio during the summer of 1863 visiting relatives and old neighbors and many friends. In the fall of 64 and during the winter I wrote the narrative of the outrages and horrors I witnessed. The sale of the book enabled me to buy a team and on the month of August I once more started for Minnesota.

My youngest brother lived in Hennepin County at that time. I arrived at his home sometimes in September. Selling books and visiting my old neighbors in Olmsted County required some time so that my journey lasted long, but I was well paid for by the warm reception from brother and family. I made my home with brother until spring of 1865 when I came to Mankato.

In the year 1866 I bought some land very cheap with money received from the United States. The kind neighbors helped me build a small frame house. And the following summer Merton built an addition-kitchen, two bedrooms and buttery, thus making a very comfortable home for the children and myself. There I lived, Merton helping what he could and being naturally ingenious, he soon learned the carpenter's trade and earned money enough with what we raised on the farm to give us a comfortable living.

The year 1870 I had an offer of marriage, which I accepted, hoping to better my condition in life. My husband was kind to my children and me. We were married but three months when he left home, unbeknown to me and went to his sister in Ohio, where he remained several days and left taking no clothing except what he wore. Neither his friends nor myself have ever heard from him and why he left or what fate I do not except to ever know, unless it is in the next world. This was a great burden to bear, but I had trouble that was still harder.

In August of 1871 I became the mother of a daughter. Merton was working at this trade, so Johnnie and myself were the ones to take care of the baby. Johnnie was ten years old but quite small, so I left him to take care of the baby and do what he could in the house. While I worked out doors, plowing, harrowing, marking and planting my ground, etc. Sometimes my neighbors helping harvest my wheat and husk my corn and helped to get my firewood until Johnnie was strong enough to do it.

In 1873 Merton was married. He was married in August and stayed home till next spring, than he went to Rochester. The following fall he wanted myself and the children to go and live with him, but I couldn't become a burden to him as long as I could get along without.

In the winter I lost one of my horses. I was not able to buy another and I had more land cleared than one horse could plow. But as I never give up in a good cause without a hard struggle, one thing I thought I might do. I owned a large cow and I thought perhaps she could make half of a team if she was broke to the harness. Well Johnnie and myself soon had her broken and had done the plowing. An odd looking team it was, but did it matter so that I accomplished the desired end that was to support my family?

Sometime in the summer of 1875 Merton wrote to me telling me that he had taken a severe cold and had been left with a cough. He wrote several letters afterward saying that all were well; but a terrible blow awaited me on the 5th of November. I received a telegram from Rochester to "come quick"

Merton is dying. Oh! What a shock. I did not faint, but I thought I should die, it was such a shock. I could not speak for some minutes; but tears, blessed tears came to my relief and then I seemed to realize the truth that Merton was dying.

I thought perhaps I might get to Rochester in time to see him once more if I made all possible haste and I accordingly went to Mankato that night and took the train next morning for Rochester. How slow the train moved! It seemed as though I could go faster myself. In my imagination I could see another train that didn't lack for speed. I knew where it would stop and what passenger would go on board.

I reached Rochester at one o'clock p. m. Mr. Joseph Alexander Jr. met me at the station. (Joe Alexander Sr. had earlier turned the crank that controlled the rollers in many of great grandfather's panorama showing) I did not need ask. I felt that Merton was gone. Mary my daughter- in-law met me at the gate, threw her arms around me kissed me and said, "Mother". She could say no more and I could say nothing, neither could I shed a tear. They told me that he begged them to do all they could to keep life in him "till mother came". He told his wife if he could see mother he would be willing to die.

He died trusting in Jesus. On Sunday I followed the remains to the grave where kind hands buried the hero of Lake Shetek my hero, the boy that carried his little brother so far and was the instrument in the hands of God in saving his life.

CHAPTER TWENTY

In 2002 Joyce and I went to the U. S. in an attempt to locate some of the Stevens and Franz old original farm sites. We also were interested in locating headstones of deceased family members who had passed on in the U. S.

We began our land search for great grandfather's Stevens original farm site in Minnesota by driving to Dodge Center. We were than directed to the larger town of Mantorville where the area's old land records were kept. It is a beautifully preserved old frontier town of mostly original stone buildings.

It was named after the Mantor Brothers, Peter and Riley who came to the area in1853 the identical year that great grandfather arrived in Rochester.

We were directed to their well-preserved old two story stone Court House in the center of town. We looked through many fragile old land record books that were stored in the basement. Eventually we were able to find great grandfather's original land location that was about ten miles south east of town

He had selected an area with excellent deep black soil more than I can say for some of my maternal ancestors. There were rows of very old Elm trees along the driveway into the farm. One wonders if my great grandparents perhaps planted them when they first arrived there.

While at Mantorville we stopped at the Dodge County Historical Society office that was located in old stone church. It is shown to the bottom left in the photo of the Court House. They indicated that anyone whose forefathers had settled there by 1875 or before was eligible to have a permanent membership in their society. We sent the necessary documentation to them and received a certificate of membership for Uncle John and myself.

Mantorville Court House featured in center of the photo

CHAPTER TWENTY-ONE

One of the original Sioux War panoramas painted by great grandfather is stored in the Minnesota History Center in St. Paul, Minnesota. How the History Center acquired this old panorama is a story of one man's persistence in his four-year search to locate one of great grandfather's original panoramas.

A Burt W. Eaton of Rochester initiated the search in 1914. As a boy growing up in Rochester he had very vivid memories of seeing great grandfather show his panorama and how large an impression it made on him. After four years of letter writing he eventually found one at Winona, Minnesota owned by a family named Horton.

Among the items recovered was the crude mechanical mechanism used to display the panorama. Also included were the wooden boxes in which the panorama was carried from town to town. Handwritten advertising and a handwritten copy of the explanatory lectures and even one of the broadsides used in advertising the panorama were included. It consisted of thirty-six panels each six feet high and seven feet wide, with an overall length of two hundred and twenty feet.

The opening panels were portraits of Lincoln and his cabinet followed by scenes from the Indian war. It concluded with panel frames of picture and events in the Black Hills, Yellowstone National Park and other scenes in the far west.

There was a Henry Horton who traveled with great grandfather in the winter panorama tour of 1873-74. We have to give great grandfather a lot of credit for hiring a colored person because of the rampant race discrimination in those frontier days. How Henry Horton acquired the panorama was never documented. This was perhaps one of the earlier panoramas that he had painted. Before it was given to the Historical Society a showing of the panorama was arranged in St. Paul in February of 1918. To add authenticity to the showing, Joe Alexander who had turned the crank forty years earlier for some of great grandfather's panorama showings was asked to perform the duty again which he did. The St. Paul Chapter of the Daughters of the American Revolution sponsored the showing and charged fifty cents for admission.

We visited the Minnesota History Center in 2002 and met with Brain Szott Curator of Art at the Center. He indicated that the old panorama was too fragile to be shown. However he did show us slides of the panorama and gave us some additional information about it.

In the 1930's a second panorama of great grandfather's with all the parts for showing it was located at Binghamton, New York supposedly owned by some of our Stevens or Donovan relatives. A New York Art Dealer Howard F. Porter of the Old Print Exchange purchased the panorama with all its equipment for a thousand dollars. In 1939 the panorama was offered to the Minnesota Historical Society for fifteen hundred dollars. Eventually it was acquired by Mr. Thomas Gilcrease of San Antonia, Texas who placed it in his private art collection in his museum near Tulsa, Oklahoma.

It consisted of thirty-six panels many of which were signed by Great Grandfather and dated Rochester 1870. Like the one great grandfather sold in 1874 this panorama was diaphanous painting. The opening frame had pictures of Minnehaha Falls; it was followed by great grandfather's favorite picture of Washington and Lafayette. These were followed by twenty-six Sioux War scenes concluding with what may be described as a newsreel of current events of the day.

The Glen Bow Museum in Calgary has one replica Panorama painting of great grandfather's. Quinn Hoag curator of the art department at the museum said it is used as illustration of early panorama's painting

CHAPTER TWENTY-TWO

We have no record of when great grandmother and her young family moved off their Minnesota farm. I have a gut feeling they headed out to South Dakota to great grandfather's land south east of Canistota. I assume they made the trip in a covered wagon no doubt taking personal belongings and some of their farm animals.

Some years later after becoming ill great grandmother may have decided to go to St. Paul Minnesota in hopes of find a cure for illness. Unfortunately on August 4th, 1883 the young family lost its last anchor with great grandmother's passing at forty-seven years of age. She passed away of stomach cancer in a boarding house not a great way to spend your final days. I find it difficult to imagine the anguish she must have felt in leaving such a young family behind. It had been just four years since great grandfather's passing. Grandfather at sixteen years old was now officially the man of the house. From what I can gather from researching old land titles Lucy grandfather's half sister helped keep the young family together after great grandmother's passing.

In a neat hand written note shown below grandfather carefully recorded the details of his mother's passing. Thanks to this information we were able to go back one hundred and nineteen years later to her exact resting place in Calvary Cemetery

Mrs. Ann J. Stevins
Died August 4th 1883
In. St. Paul Minn.
At No. 232 East 7th Street
Grave No 1 in Block 22 in sec24
Calvary Cemetery
In Saint Paul
Burried August 11th 1883
Mother was 47 years 3 months
an 3 days old.

Calvary Cemetery is a beautiful old well cared for cemetery located in down town St. Paul, Minnesota. When grandma and I visited the cemetery in 2002 a very kind gentleman from the staff took us to the exact spot of her original gravesite. It was located underneath a beautiful large old oak tree. There was no evidence of a head stone; no doubt the wooden cross that was used had long since succumbed to the elements.

Grandma Joyce Stevens standing under an old oak tree close to great grandmother's original gravesite

CHAPTER TWENTY-THREE

Eighty years after great grandfathers passing some of his panorama scenes appeared in the May 1959 issue of Life Magazine. It was part of a continuing series on "How the West was Won" it featured a pictorial journey of how the west evolved as seen through the eyes of early American artist's.

How our family was even aware of the feature article in Life could be described as one of those chance encounters that sometimes occur in life. Cousin Fee Otterson was taking a Sabbatical at Notre Dame University in South Bend, Indiana in 1959. Apparently a copy of that issue of Life magazine had been left in the men bathroom. Much to Fee's surprise he noticed the photo's and references to great grandfather John Stevens early panorama paintings included in the May issue of Life.

It featured dramatic scenes of the conflicts of the American Indians attempting to defend their hunting grounds against the early settlers. It also showed how the early cattle developed the folklore that surrounds the cowboy drives across the plains. Included in the lead page was a photo of great grandfather seated in his Rochester studio. It also featured a large painting from his Sioux War Panorama.

Great Grandfather John Stevens in his Rochester studio

DEATH RIDES UP on a homesteader threshing wheat near St. Peter, 30 miles east of the Sioux reservation. The Indians killed and scalped this man and seven others who were working with him. The uprising began and spread so swiftly that settlers, unwarned and unarmed, had no chance to fight back. After the attack, local citizens quickly formed a militia unit, the St. Peter Frontier Guards, armed with clubs, pitchforks and a few single-barrel shotguns.

FLEEING WHITES at Lake Shetek were cut down by the Sioux. Lavinia East-lick, holding the reins, was shot four times but escaped alive. Three of her five sons were clubbed to death. At least 14 men, women and children were killed.

CHAPTER TWENTY-FOUR

The series on How the West was Won in Life magazine prompted a Sioux Falls, South Dakota news paper to interview grandfather's sister Kate. In their story there was a picture of her holding a self-portrait of her father that he painted using a mirror. A large photo is shown hanging to her left of great grandmother no doubt painted by great grandfather also. Unfortunately we do not have any photos of our great grandmother Ann Stevens.

Following are two original paintings of great grandfather that belong to our family. My grandmother had them on display on the south wall of her dining room.

One was a self-portrait of great grandfather and the other was his portrait painting of the famous General Custer. The writing on the rear of the photo shown below indicates the photo was used as part of the advertising in promoting great grandfather's panorama depicting General Custer's last stand. Cousin Larry McGillis now has General Custer's photo on display in his basement recreational room.

Undated Self Portrait of great grandfather John Stevens

General George Custer

CHAPTER TWENTY-FIVE

In February of 2006 I received a surprise package in the mail of a copy of the original title to great grandfather's farm at Dodge Center from cousin Fee Otterson. How the old land certificate survived some one hundred thirty years before re surfacing is an interesting story.

Great grandmother must have taken it with her when they left their Minnesota farm. Upon her death grandfather acquired the title and kept it with him for years. When grandfather passed on it was left with grandma. When grandma passed on Aunt Margaret acquired it and it was with her keepsakes. With Aunt Margaret's passing Fee acquired some of her keepsakes. Fee was going through some of her papers recently and discovered it. Not quite sure of the significance of it to our family history Fee sent it to me. Starting with my great grandmother Anne Stevens I am the sixth person to have it in their possession.

WARRANTEE DEED.

FROM

W. E. Fairbank &
Wife

TO

John Stevens

OFFICE OF REGISTER OF DEEDS.

STATE OF MINNESOTA,
County of *Dodge,* } ss.

I hereby certify that the within Deed was filed in this Office for record on the ...... day of ......
A. D. 187_ at ...... o'clock ...... M., and was duly recorded in Book ...... of Deeds, on page ......
....
Register of Deeds.
....
.... *Deputy.*

Entered for Transfer. Taxes .... Paid.

.... *March 26th* ...... 187_
.... *Auditor,*
.... *Dodge* ...... County, Minnesota.

Dear Jack:

How this came into my mother's possession I do not know.

Take care!

Lee

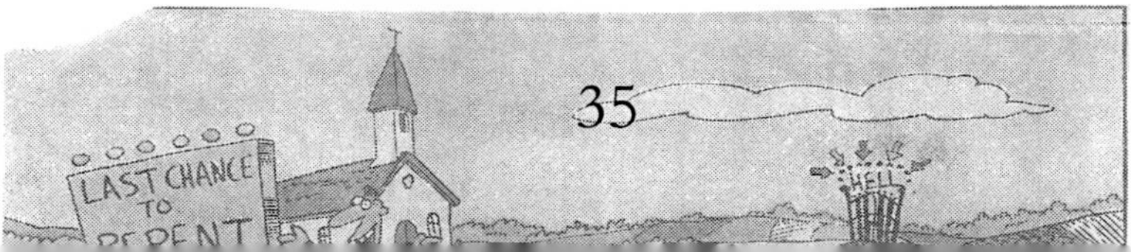

35

Dear Jack:
    How this came into
my mother's possession
I do not know.

    Take care!

            Joe

Saint Felix — Patron Saint of Procrastinators.

CHAPTER TWENTY-SIX

As mentioned previously in the prologue great grandfather Jacob Franz began an odyssey as a teenager in Southern Germany in the late 1850's eventually arriving in the United States some time prior to 1861.

On August 14th, 1861 just four months after the declaration of war between the North and the South, at the age of nineteen he joined Company H second Regiment, Iowa Cavalry of the Union Army at Davenport, Iowa. On his enlistment papers his occupation was listed as butcher and his height six feet. We may have inherited some of the Stevens family genes for extra height from great grandfather Franz.

The Civil War was one of the few wars in history that was fought over mostly principle not territory. The North wanted to free the Negroes from slavery and the South was opposed; fortunately the North was victorious. Interestingly if the American Revolution of 1776 had been delayed by a few years The British Parliament by abolishing slavery would have become law in their American colony. This may have prevented the loss of 700,000 lives in the Civil War.

Three years and five months later on October 3rd, 1864 great grandfather was discharged from the army for medical reasons receiving a pension of three dollars a month. Medical problems originating from his Civil war service would plague great grandfather Franz for his remaining years.

CHAPTER TWENTY-SEVEN

Five months later on March 9th, 1865 great grandfather married an Irish girl named Mary O'Donnell at Iowa City, Iowa. Great grandmother had been born in the City of Limerick in Ireland on April 5th 1842. Great grandfather was twenty-three and great grandmother twenty years old when they were married. According to a Department of the Interior, Bureau of Pensions questionnaire that great grandfather Franz filled out on June 16th 1898 Justice Dotter officiated at their wedding ceremony. He also indicated at that time their original marriage certificate had been destroyed by fire.

Eight of their nine children were born at Marengo including my grandmother Mary who was born there on May 29th, 1868. Three of the Franz children passed away while the family was living at Marengo. A little girl named Louise at three years old, Charles also at three years and a little baby Charles the second at one year old

Grandma was seven at the time of Louise passing, eight when Charles died and eleven when her baby brother Charles passed on. The strong life time family bond that grandma and her remaining siblings had was no doubt reinforced by their childhood memories of how precious family and life can be.

Grandma's oldest sister Cecilia Miller recorded the following two pages of the Jacob Franz family births and deaths. Frank Collins noted she made some errors in spelling however we would have to give her credit for recording this important information. By the handwriting I assume it was done in the later years of her life.

Deaths   Marengo Iowa.
Louisa Christina Franz December 9th 1875
Charles Frederick   „   Jan.   11-1876
Charles Frederick 2d   „   Feb.   1878
Timothy   „   Aug.   17 1884

Mother
Mary Franz   March 7- 1893.
at Salem, S.D. age 47 years 11 months 2 days
Father
Jonathan Jacob Franz Sr. Feb. 11-1900. at
Edmonton Canada (Alberta) N. W. T. age 58 years
1 month and 9 days
Edward Henry Franz March, 15 1917
at Wilmar, Minn. on the train. buried
at Salem S.D.
John J. Franz Jr June 12-1931
Edmonton, Alberta Canada 61 years age

CHAPTER TWENTY-EIGHT

In 1880 perhaps wanting to start a new life the family left Iowa. They followed the frontier westward on the Chicago and Northwestern railroad as they pushed their rail lines westward towards the then Dakota Territory. We think great grandfather obtained work helping supply meat to the hundreds of men involved in the construction of the railway. His occupation was listed as a butcher while the family lived in Marengo. According to some of my German friends in the mid 1800 hundreds the apprenticeship for learning the butcher trade began at age fourteen in Germany. When the railway reached Woonsockett in the Dakota Territory the family decided to end their vagabond life and put down roots.

The new frontier towns always had a large population of single men looking for lodging and food. With this in mind my great grandparents started a combination butcher shop, bakery and boarding house. With great grandfather Franz's butchering skills and great grandmother and family doing the cooking they did well. Grandma's excellent baking and cooking skills no doubt were honed from helping in the family boarding house. Uncle John Franz besides being an excellent carpenter was equally proficient as a butcher. Skills no doubt he acquired from the time the family ran their butcher shop in Woonsocket.

CHAPTER THIRTY

The ultimate dream of the majority of the individuals who followed the frontier west was to become landowners. In 1885 my great grandparents accomplished this dream. They bought or took over the mortgage on a farm some thirty miles southeast of Woonsocket, South Dakota. The terms were a dollar down and they took over a mortgage of eight hundred and seventy eight dollars payable to a Loan and Trust Company. There was no mention of interest charges or terms. Great grandfather's credit must have been good to negotiate such small down payment. The farm they selected was ten miles southeast of Canistota with the Vermillion River running through the western part of their farm. In addition to the original one hundred and seventy eight acres great grandfather purchased an adjoining forty acres for fifty dollars.

WARRANTY DEED RECORD.

This Indenture, Made the ___7th___ day of ___October___ in the year of our Lord One Thousand Eight Hundred and Eighty ___Five___ by and between ___Jacob Franz___

of the county of ___McCook___ in the Territory of Dakota, party of the first part, and ___Mary Franz___

of the County of ___McCook___ in the Territory of Dakota, party of the second part, Witnesseth, That the said party of the first part, for and in consideration of the sum of ___One___

_____ DOLLARS to ___her___ in hand paid by the said party of the second part, the receipt whereof is hereby acknowledged, ha ___?___ granted, bargained, sold and conveyed, and by these presents do ___?___ grant, bargain, sell and convey unto the said party of the second part, and to ___her___ heirs and assigns forever, all ___that___ certain piece or parcel of land situate in the County of McCook and Territory of Dakota, described as follows, to-wit:

The East half of the North West Quarter and the West half of the North East Quarter and the North East quarter of the North East Quarter of Section Number Fourteen (14) in Township One Hundred and One (101) North of Range Fifty Three (53) West 5th P.M.

Together with, all and singular, the hereditaments and appurtenances thereunto belonging or in anywise appertaining

TO HAVE AND TO HOLD the said premises with the appurtenances to the said party of the second part ___her___ ____ and assigns forever, and the said ___Jacob Franz___ ____ for ___him___ self ___ and ___her___ heirs, executors and administrators do covenant and agree to and with the said party of the second part ___her___ ____ heirs and assigns, that ___he is___ ____ well seized in fee of the lands and premises aforesaid, and ha ___?___ good right and lawful authority to sell and convey the same in manner and form aforesaid; and the same are free from all incumbrances whatsoever ____ ____

IN WITNESS WHEREOF, the said part ___y___ of the first part ha ___?___ hereunto set ___her___ hand ____ and seal the day and year first above written.

Signed and delivered in presence of

E. W. Coughran }

Jacob Franz (Seal.)
_____ (Seal.)
_____ (Seal.)
_____ (Seal.)

Territory of Dakota, County of ___Minnehaha___ ss.

BE IT REMEMBERED, That on this ___8th___ day of ___October___ in the year One Thousand Eight Hundred and Eighty ___Five___ before me ___E. W. Coughran___ ____ Notary Public ____ within and for said county and Territory personally appeared ___Jacob Franz___

____ well known to me to be the person ____ who ___is___ ____ described in and who executed the within and foregoing instrument, and severally duly acknowledged to me that ___he___ executed the same freely.

IN WITNESS WHEREOF, I have hereunto set my hand and official seal at said County the day and year above written.

(Seal)

E. W. Coughran
Notary Public, Minnehaha Co. D.T.

Filed for record this ___2d___ day of ___Nov.___ 1885 at 11 o'clock and ___?___ minutes ___A.M.___
and recorded on page ___94___ Book H.

E. H. Smith

At the time of their move to the farm great uncle Ed Franz was twenty years old however a childhood accident had left him severely disabled. As we mentioned previously great grandfather had serious ongoing health problems resulting from his Army service. Great grandmother Franz also had suffered with serious circulation problems in her legs for many years. As a result of their parents serious health challenges I would have to assume the remaining Franz siblings contributed a lot to the successful running of their new farm. Considering the hard work grandma did on the farm as a young girl her love of the land and farming would remain with her for the rest of her life.

Several years after their move to the farm a young local farm boy named Casper Miller married grandma's oldest sister Cecilia. The Miller family would farm in the immediate Canistota area for their remaining years. Grandma always affectionately referred to her older sister Cecilia as Ceal.

CHAPTER THIRTY-ONE

Grandfather John Stevens and his siblings were farming in the immediate area when the Franz family moved to their new farm in 1885. No doubt the two remaining Franz girls did not go unnoticed by the unmarried young men of the district. A serious relationship began to develop between grandma and grandfather. There was however one very dark cloud one the horizon that threatened to derail their future relationship.

Great Grandfather Franz was less than impressed with this young Irish farm neighbor boy. He was reported to have said to grandma, "You aren't going to marry that Irishman are you?" Grandfather was only half Irish however he must have inherited a lot of Irish genes and mannerisms from his Irish mother. The prevailing sentiment at the time certainly did not favor the Irish. It was common to see notices in store windows particularly in the bigger cities back east that read, "No Irish need apply". As we previously discussed most of the Irish Catholics from Ireland came to America more like fleeing refugees than normal immigrants as a result of hundreds years of enslavement by their English masters.

42

Grandma was a very strong willed person and thankfully did not take her father's advice. How events unfolded which resulted in the ultimate marriage of my grandparents was related to me by Cousin Gertrude Bohan. Grandma told the story to Gertrude while they were sitting at the Otterson kitchen nook in their home a few years prior to her passing.

Grandfather realizing that grandma and his proposed marriage plans had reached an impasse took matters into his own hands. One morning while grandma was out feeding the pigs on their farm she had a very important visitor in the person of grandfather. His message to grandma was "Mame the Catholic priest is scheduled to be in town today and we should go get married". And as they say the rest is history. My grandparents were married that day November 9th, 1899 at Canistota.

As we indicated earlier grandfather had purchased his father's original land near Canistota. I would have to assume that my grandparents lived on this farm after their marriage.

CHAPTER THIRTY-TWO

Approximately a year later on December 6th, 1890 Aunt Irene was born the first of the five girls that eventually would be part of the John and Mary Stevens family.

In 1891 my grandparents purchased my great grandparents Franz two hundred acre farm. It is interesting to note on the title transfer shown below that great grandmother signed her name with x. This was referred to on the title transfer as her mark. In their many invasions of Ireland the English ruled with an iron hand. The children of the Irish tenant farmers were forbidden to attend school. We would have to assume that my great grandmother Franz never had the opportunity to attend school.

In January of 1892 my grandparents sold the original Stevens farm for the excellent sum of fifteen hundred dollars. However the big event of 1892 in the Stevens household was the arrival of another girl Margaret Anne on November 4th.

Following is a duplicate copy of the 1891 Warranty Deed of the sale of the Franz farm to grandfather John Stevens.

Stevens

<table>
<tr><td>

WARRANTY DEED.

Mary Hrany & Husband

TO

John D. Stevens

TERRITORY OF DAKOTA, } ss.
County of McCook,

I hereby certify that the within Deed was filed in this office for Record on the 4th day of Jany A.D. 1872 at 2 o'clock P.M., and was duly recorded in book K of Deeds, page 121.

Jerry Bennitt
Register of Deeds.

</td><td>

This Indenture, Made this 21st day of December

in the year of our Lord one thousand eight hundred and Sixty One between Mary Hrany and Jacob Hrany wife & husband of the County of McCook and State of South Dakota part of the first part, and John D. Stevens of the County, and Cook and State of South Dakota part y of the second part, WITNESSETH, that the said part ies of the first part, in consideration of the sum of Two hundred and No/100 DOLLARS, to them in hand paid by the said part y of the second part, the receipt whereof is hereby acknowledged, do hereby GRANT, BARGAIN, SELL AND CONVEY unto the said part y of the second part, his heirs and assigns, FOREVER, all a tract or parcel of land, lying and being in the County of McCook and State of South Dakota, described as follows, to wit: the East half (E½) of the North West (N W⁴) Quarter and the West half (W½) of the North East quarter (N E¼) and the North East quarter (N E¼) of the North East qr (N E¼) all in Section Number fourteen (14) in Township one hundred and one (101) North of Range

</td></tr>
</table>

Fifty three (53) West of the 5th P.M. containing two hundred acres more or less according to the Government Survey thereof

TO HAVE AND TO HOLD THE SAME, Together with all the hereditaments and appurtenances thereunto belonging or in anywise appertaining, to the said part y of the second part, his heirs and assigns FOREVER. And the said Mary Hrany and Jacob Hrany administrators, do covenant with the said part y of the second part, his heirs and assigns, that they are well seized in fee of the lands and premises aforesaid, and ha ve good right to sell and convey the same in manner and form aforesaid ; that the same are free from all incumbrances; except as shown by the County records.

and the above bargained and granted lands and premises, in the quiet and peaceable possession of the said part y of the second part, his heirs and assigns, against all persons lawfully claiming or to claim the whole or any part thereof, the said part ies of the first part will WARRANT AND DEFEND.

IN TESTIMONY WHEREOF, The said part y of the first part hereunto set their hand s and seal s the day and year first above written.

Signed, Sealed and Delivered in Presence of

A. C. Biernatzki

J. C. Hradle

                                        her
                              Mary + Hrany   [SEAL]
                                   mark
                                                [SEAL]
                              Jacob Hrany   [SEAL]
                                                [SEAL]

TERRITORY OF SOUTH DAKOTA, } ss.
County of McCook,

On this 21st day of December in the year one thousand eight hundred and Ninety one Before me A. C. Biernatzki, Judge of County Court in the said County and State personally came Mary Hrany and Jacob Hrany wife & husband known to me to be the persons who executed the foregoing instrument and acknowledged to me that they executed the same

[SEAL]

to me well known as the same persons described in and who executed the foregoing Deed, and acknowledged that he executed the same freely and voluntarily.

And the said who is described as a married woman in and whose name is subscribed to the within and foregoing instrument, upon an examination without the hearing of her husband, being by me made acquainted with the contents of the said instrument, thereupon acknowledged to me that she executed the same freely, and that she did not wish to retract such execution.

IN WITNESS WHEREOF, I have hereunto set my hand and official seal at said county, the day and year above written.

A. C. Biernatzki, Judge of the County Court

CHAPTER THIRTY-THREE

Great grandmother problems with her legs continued to get worse which eventually required one of her legs to be amputated in late 1892. Four doctors at the Franz home performed the operation. The family kitchen was converted to an operating room with the surgery being performed on the kitchen table. We would have to assume in that era kitchen tables were large and very well constructed.

An old letter sent to Andy and Myra Morin by Cousin Frank Collins who was grandma's sister Alice's son confirmed this fact. Frank made the following comment on great grandmother's obituary notice that had been sent to him by Cousin Marcella Jesse. In his note Frank refers to Mabel Jesse who was a daughter of grandma's sister Ceal. "Mabel Jesse said that those days they called grandma's condition Milk Leg. Mabel was there at Grandma's when the surgery took place. She was peeking and watched. The kitchen table was the operating table, a very common practice those days. I believe now days they would call it diabetes".

Mabel Jesse no doubt would have spent time at her grandparents Franz home in Salem. Mom kept in touch with both Mabel and her daughter Marcella. I have an old letter of Mabel's that she sent to Mom and Dad on June 27th 1974. Among other things she indicated that she had recently celebrated her 86th birthday on May 31st of that year. According to that information Mabel would have been five years old when her grandmother Franz had her leg amputated at home on their kitchen table.

The following obituary notice of great grandmother Franz passing was in the Salem Semi Weekly Special March 8th 1893.

Mrs. Jacob Franz who suffered the amputation of one of her legs sometime ago died yesterday morning. Her enfeebled condition caused by her sixteen years of constant suffering had reached that state where insufficient vitality remained to withstand the shock of the operation. Mrs. Franz was comparatively a new comer, having lived here about a year. In this time she made many warm friends. She was universally respected and admired for her thrift and industry and many kind and noble traits of character. She was a faithful member of the Catholic Church and died peacefully in the hope of a glorious resurrection. The Special extends its sympathy to the bereaved family in the hour of their affliction.

Frank made the following comment regarding great grandmother's death notice. "The type setter those days made mistakes also Re resurrection". I note whoever wrote the column also misspelled comparatively. However we would have to give the writer an A for effort in the descriptive wording used in great grandmother's obituary notice.

Frank also made the following notation, "St. Mary's church records show she died March 6th buried March 8th cause blood poison". St. Mary's present Catholic Church is a beautiful stone building that was constructed in the early 1900's. The article below was among grandma Stevens's keepsakes regarding the surgery performed on her mother.

Mrs. Jacob Franz who has suffered for years with some disease affecting one of her limbs, and last Monday the diseased member was amputated above the knee, Drs. Peterman of Parker, Cummings of Montrose and Beveriqge of Bridgewater assisting our local physiceans Drs. Ware and Edgerton in the operation. The lady is getting along as well as can be expected, and it is hoped will soon be in tne enjoyment of perfect health.

Great grandmother was born in the City of Limerick in Southern Ireland at the height of the potato famine. Like thousands of others no doubt her family fled Ireland hoping for better life in North America.

Great grandmother's final resting place is in the well-maintained St. Mary's Catholic Church cemetery out on the Dakota prairie west of Salem. One of the unique things about her head stone is that it is round and the lettering is perfectly preserved after hundred plus years. Frank Collins had taken the excellent photo of her headstone below perhaps twenty years prior to our visiting the cemetery in 2002.

Great Grandmother (Mary) Franz Salem, S. D. 1892

CHAPTER THIRTY-FOUR

In the following chapter we will update the later fortunes of the Franz family and that of the growing family of John and Mary Stevens.

Several years after his mother's passing, Uncle John Franz was away working at Bolite, Kansas. We have a nice photo of him in a firemen's uniform with a buttoner in his lapel dated 1895 at Bolite, Kansas. The photo was in the form of a Post Card and was sent home to his younger sister Alice at Canistota.

We would have to assume that grandma's sister Alice stayed home after her mother's death to housekeep for great grandfather and her brother Ed. In

1897 Alice married Harry Collins and they went to live on his farm just east of Canistota. The photo following is a photo I assume was taken of Alice and Harry on or shortly after their marriage.

On November 23, 1894 my grandparents' third daughter Mary Mae was born. Several years later in 1896 a photo of the young family was taken at the Sam Beddoe studio in Canistota.

Aunt Irene and Aunt Margaret are sitting beside grandfather with Aunt Mae seated on his lap. Aunt Mae's facial expressions indicate she was not thrilled with the photo session. My grandparents also had individual portraits taken at the same time. Grandfather would have been twenty-nine and grandma twenty-eight at the time of their studio photo session.

On December 7th, 1897 another girl Kathryn Agnes was added to the John and Mary Stevens family. Grandfather was perhaps beginning to feel slightly inferior with the increasing number of the girls now in the Stevens household.

CHAPTER THIRTY-FIVE

In the late summer of 1899 great grandfather Franz embarked on what would be the final journey of his life to Edmonton, Alberta. He would have crossed the North Saskatchewan River on John Walters Ferry the Belle. It would be two years into the future before the Low Level Bridge was built across the North Saskatchewan River.

As we previously discussed great grandfather's health was fragile at the best of times as a result of conditions he endured while serving in the Civil War. He was discharged from the Army for medical reasons with a monthly pension of three dollars. This was increased to six dollars a month in the last few years of his life. Shortly after arriving in Edmonton he became ill and passed away the following February 11th, 1900 at the General Hospital far away from friends and family.

The following item appeared I presume in the Edmonton Bulletin under the obituary notices.

Franz- at Edmonton on Sunday, the 11th 1900 Jacob Franz aged 58 years. Funeral takes place on Wednesday at 2 p. m. from Hourston's Hall.

Jacob Franz who came here from South Dakota last summer, died in the hospital here yesterday, after somewhat of lingering illness. The deceased was an elderly man, 58 years of age and leaves a grown- up family in the States. He was a Grand Army veteran and a member of the I.O.O.F. under whose auspices the funeral was conducted. The funeral leaves Hourston's Hall on Wednesday at 2 p. m.

When we examine great grandfather's Franz life he no doubt like all other immigrants faced a language and other barriers after arriving in the U. S. One is left to wonder if one of his reasons for his coming to the U. S. was to avoid service in the German Army. However events would prove otherwise as far as avoiding military service once arriving in the United States. Health problems would plague him for his remaining years as the result of his Army service.

Like many other immigrants great grandfather married a young lady who was also a native of a far away land. Together through hard work and thrift they established a business and eventually purchased a farm. They were able to see the second generation take over their land. They even moved to town in their retirement years however they would not enjoy it long together with great grandmother passing away a year later.

After having been a widower for six years and with his youngest daughter Alice now married great grandfather perhaps felt at loose ends. In late 1899 he embarked on what would be his last journey of discovery to Canada. Whether he hoped to buy land or report back on the opportunities available for work to his two sons we will never know.

While in Edmonton his ongoing health problems intervened and he passed away in a strange land far away from family and friends. A simple flat headstone marks great grandfather's Franz final resting place in the Edmonton Cemetery.

Shortly after great grandfather's passing grandfather John Stevens traveled to Edmonton which in 1900 was just a small frontier town. Satisfied with grandfather's plot location and I assume carry a few of his personal items he returned home. However the seed had been planted in grandfather's mind of the potential of this vast untamed frontier.

CHAPTER THIRTY-SIX

Cousin Frank Collins did extensive research on great grandfather's Franz Civil War records. He also documented his long and successful effort to have his monthly Army disability pension adjusted. Frank sent copies of these documents plus others to cousins Andy and Myra Morin years ago. They have graciously passed Frank's extensive documentation efforts on to me.

I think it is important that we look at some of the information that Frank was successful in obtaining. As I alluded to earlier great grandfather was plagued with serious health problems his entire life which began during his Army service.

He was first hospitalized for eight months between August 1862 and March 1863 at an Army hospital in northern Mississippi at Rienzi. The cause of his illness was severe diarrhea which obviously they were having a difficult time treating. Later he was again hospitalized for the same condition in an Army hospital at Corinth in northern Mississippi. His last hospitalization prior to his discharge in 1864 was at Mount Pleasant, Illinois and Keokut, Iowa with no length of stay given.

Great grandfather, in a document dated July 1882 and referred to as The Declaration for an Original Invalid Pension, detailed all the above information. The purpose of which was to apply for an additional monthly pension allowance. Apparently the United States Pension Agency required additional proof of his disability. After a time lapse of two years he received a reply from the Army Pension office. They requested two General Affidavits to be submitted by two persons known to great grandfather verifying indeed he did have ongoing chronic health problems.

They also requested that he supply his official discharge papers from the United States Army. He indicated that they had been destroyed in a fire. Before the Army could proceed with his additional monthly pension request a duplicate copy was issued on August 27th, 1877 that is shown below.

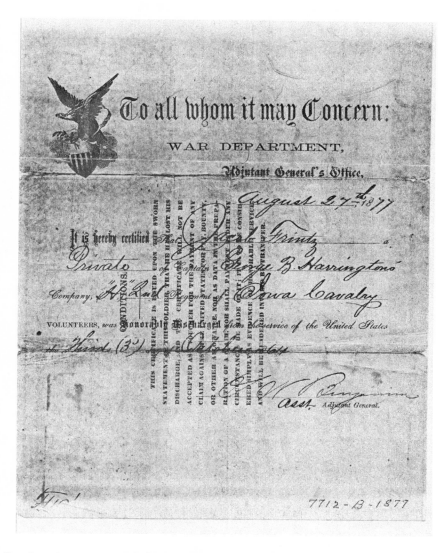

Following is a copy of the General Affidavit that Grandfather filled out before a Notary Public on July 6th 1894. The other General Affidavit was submitted by grandfather's brother in law Casper Miller basically giving the same facts that grandfather did in his Affidavit.

55

Grandfather's Affidavit was filled out on July 6th 1894 with grandfather giving his age as twenty-eight. Grandfather wrote the following." I have lived neighbor to the claimant from 1885 until 1893. Have changed farm work with him and known that during that time he, the claimant complained much and was unable to perform manual labor to the extent of ½. And I know that the ailment which was general debility and chronic diarrhea was not caused by vicious habits".

Eight months later On March 8th 1895 the United States Pension Agency did grant great grandfather an increase of three dollars to his current monthly pension allowance. I admired his persistence in pursuing what he rightly thought was his legitimate claim to additional pension funds. Frank obtained a copy of a receipt of eighteen dollars covering great grandfather's Army pension from December 4th 1899 to March 4th 1900 issued by the Pension Agent at Washington D. C.

One has to wonder if these additional pension funds helped cover some of the expenses of great grandfather Franz's last exploratory journey to Western Canada in late 1899.

Great Grandfather Franz circa 1892

Great grandfather's flat headstone at the Edmonton Cemetery

The remains of the Late Bro Treanty.
are Interred in the IOOF
plot. Block 4 Edmund's Cemetary
in Lot I situated in the North
West corner thereof.

JM Clark
Sec

CHAPTER THIRTY-SEVEN

The following is a copy of "The Old Settlers Picnic" written by Aunt Mae recalling her experiences as young girl on the farm in Dakota. I would guess the time period she is referring to would be around 1900. The photo below of the four Stevens girls would closely resemble how they appeared when they accompanied their parents on that long ago Saturday to the Old Settlers picnic.

Aunt Mae made the following comment prior to beginning her story, "the common deeds of the common day are the ringing bells in the far away"

The gladness in doing tasks at hand fixed in my childhood by my father never changed throughout my long life. It has given me a feeling of security that untold wealth could not equal. It was the little happinesses, the modest joys that made our world go round. Reminiscing... I remember especially the Old Settlers Picnic.

I can still sense the excitement that flashed through me like chain lightening before a sudden summer storm when father came home from town with the news that the day was set for the old Settlers picnic. Oh happy day the highlight of our summer was near at hand.

Our river valley farm straddled the East Vermillion River, some ten miles from Canistota where at the edge of town Howard's Grove, the annual mid-summer picnic was held. At that time it was the weather that pretty well commanded the activities of the farmer. So I prayed with all the fervor of monk in his monastery that God would grace the day with sunshine. Aware of my concern, I so well remember how father would gaze intently up at the sky, sniff the air then note the direction of the wind and say "sure as you're born it's going to be a lovely day for the picnic".

The kitchen became a hive of activity. Mother's famous golden crusted buns fresh from the oven filled the room with their delicious aroma and vied for space beside the stacks of fat raisin studded cookies on the cooling racks.

It was nearly suppertime before Mother got around to making the ice cream. Father had brought the ice in from the icehouse before he went out to the field at noon. It was partly smashed setting in a tub beside the freezer north of the house and tightly covered with heavy brown gunnysacks. I could scarcely wait for the freezing to start for when the cream was frozen Mother would lift the beater from the can and hand it to us children to lick. No ice cream could compare with mother's brand of vanilla-lemon.

After supper came our baths and shampoos and off to bed we were sent. All four of us.... Irene, Margaret, Kathryn and myself. To bed to dream of the big day just beyond the next sunrise. When morning came we woke to Mother's call, "Girls, breakfast is ready." Down the stairs we raced in our long white nightgowns. As we flew through the door there stood father, grinning from ear to ear. "Hurrah for the picnic", and immediately burst into sung and dance a lively Irish jig. My delight was almost too great to bear.

After breakfast I went with mother to the chicken yard to feed and water the baby chicks. A gnarled old willow tree leaned low over the brooder pens. There in the cool mottled shade the mother hens clucked and scratched, each surrounded by her own brood. Father watered the horses and turned them out to pasture for the day. All but Prince and Colonel, they would be hitched to the double buggy with the bright red wheels and take us to the picnic.

For picnics and Sunday afternoon visiting amongst our more distant neighbors, Mother always dressed us in our second best. Our best was reserved for wear at Mass on Sundays. Those dresses were made of fine white muslin and trimmed with rows and rows of lace. Mother was a fine seamstress and made every stitch we wore.

Upstairs to dress for the picnic we found our clothes laid out in neat rows on top of one of the beds. Lace- edged panties and two ruffled petticoats for each of us lay beside four little chambray dresses... two pink and two blue. Close by were four pairs of black patent leather slippers. Our hats were beautiful, Aunt Kate, (Grandfather's youngest sister) who was learning the millinery trade in Sioux Falls, made them for us. She fashioned them from some gossamer material in pastel shades of ink and blue, over shapes that framed our faces in the poke bonnet style and trimmed them with tiny clusters of pink and blue for-get-me-nots. Matching ribbons were tied in bows beneath our chins.

When the chores were finished father hitched Prince and Colonel to the buggy and loaded the picnic hampers and ice cream freezer into the space behind the back seat. Mother, father and Kathryn took their places on the front seat and Irene, Margaret and me on the back seat. Much to my dislike I always had to sit in the middle. "All aboard", father called and away we went.

The drive to and from the picnic grounds was as exciting experience. Would Prince shy at some imaginary object when crossing the low-walled stone bridge at the foot of the hill? Would he drag us all over the wall into the river below?

When we passed the Dutchman's place we craned our necks hoping to see his children outside playing in the yard dressed in jodhpurs and wooden shoes. A little further along set way back from the road was a towering solitary tree. Every time we passed that spot we waited silently for father to say, "My mother planted that tree". The tree was the only tangible evidence we had of our grandmother, whom we had never seen and had answered the call shortly after the Civil War to, "Go west". But of all places we passed, the 'mystery' excited our curiosity the most. There lived children that had two mothers. A small herd of goats gamboled about all over the place. Never had we seen goats before. The people that lived there were Mormons.

Uncle Harry and Aunt Alice had a booth on the grounds. The stand was made from new sweet smelling lumber with leafy green boughs criss-crossed overhead for shade. Planks placed on two sides served as seats. There tired mothers trailing tiny tots rested and chatted while enjoying a five or ten cent dish of ice cream or a glass of ice cold lemonade.

We always shared are lunch with Aunt Alice and family so immediately after we arrived we checked with them and decided on a spot where the shade was just right and not to far from their stand. Once a place was chosen the checked tablecloths were taken off the food hampers and spread end to end on the short green grass to form a table down the center. Mother and Aunt Alice placed large plates overflowing with the most delicious food. All home cooked but the picnic oranges.
Father placed a blanket on the grass at one end of the festive board for mother and Aunt Alice to sit on kitty- cornered from each other. From their vantage point they kept an eye on the children and chatted cozily all through the meal. It was in this setting that I learned about appendicitis 'Appendeseedis' Aunt Alice called it.

Luncheon was over but Mother and Aunt Alice remained in their places for extra cups of tea. Green tea. Aunt Alice had just lifted the heavy granite teapot to refill their cups when she caught sight of a little girl about my age hippity hopping along beside her mother. Setting the teapot down she froze in silence and the child and her mother were beyond earshot. Then in a stirring voice said, "That's the little Lynden girl, Mame. That's the little girl I was telling you about. Remember"? Much to Aunt Alice's chagrin it was plain to see Mother didn't remember.

"That's the little tyke that had the operation for appendiseedis" "No", gasped Mother setting down her cup heavily. "That's right. That's Lisa Lynden", emphasized Aunt Alice with a vigorous nod of her head as she poured more tea. Then continued, "Swallowing seeds whole, that's what causes appendeseedis". "Now Alice," cautioned Mother, "Are you sure"? "Absolutely…Positively" I was overwhelmed. I was a seed swallower. I had been warned time and time again that a tree might grow in my tummy. But none ever had. But this new danger called "appende-seed-us". I was scared and for the moment I couldn't forget the lemon seed in my tummy that had slipped down with my lemonade during lunch. Then Oh heavenly days, the carousel started.

The hypnotic sound of the calliope piping the old familiar tune, "Reading and Writing and Rithmetic", floated over on the soft summer breeze as round and round the painted ponies raced with wide flaring nostrils, high arched necks and long flowing tails. When the barker called; "Hurry, hurry, hurry, get your tickets here. Five cents a ride. Six for a quarter" father with a twinkle in his eye sauntered over and escorted his jubilant young daughters to the merry-go-round.

I walked on the giddy edge of intoxication for the merry-go round was the great love of my young life. I would select one special pony maybe because it was a high stepping brindled charger, or just because it was a dappled grey. Whatever the reason for my choice, that certain pony was mine for the day and I would ride on no other.

By the time the baseball games were over, races run and the last horseshoe pitched, the sun was setting low in the west. It was then the village band, resplendent in their scarlet and gold uniforms, took their places on the stage in the pavilion and started tuning their instruments in readiness to play for the dancing soon to begin.

Looking back now I know that sound was the signal that sent parents of the very young scurrying about to collect their children and head for home. The same sound brought out the young men and their ladies in droves to parade the grounds until the music of the first dance called them to the dance floor.

What a wonderful day… a day to remember…a day to cherish.

FOOT NOTE

According to information published in Within Our Borders a history of McCook County South Dakota, The Old Settlers Picnic was held annually on the second Saturday in June. The picnic was moved to the town of Canistota and renamed the Sport's Day after the last 1906 Old Settlers Picnic. The first Sport's Day in Canistota was held on July 26th 1907. It had all the many activities that Aunt Mae described in her recollections of this enjoyable summer event. An estimated twenty five hundred people attended the 1907 Sport Day. The day's activities ended with the traditional dance in the evening. I am sure the Stevens family was among the many who were in attendance at the July 26th Sports Day in 1907.

Aunt Mae mentions grandfather's sister Kate was learning the Millinery trade in Sioux Falls. She apparently had made the Stevens girls hats they wore to the Old Settlers picnic. We have a nice undated portrait of Kate and her husband George Roth shown below taken on their wedding day at Sioux Falls, South Dakota.

CHAPTER THIRTY-EIGHT

On December 5th, 1904 a baby boy who they named John was added to my grandparent's family. What excitement the first boy in a family of four girls and to top it off, he arrived on his dad's birthday. As a middle name they choose the patron saint of farmers St. Isidore who looked after Dad very well for all his many years of farming. The following announcement was in a Canistota newspaper.

S. Peters was up from Spring Valley Township Wednesday afternoon and informed us that a great big boy had made his appearance at the home of Mr. and Mrs. John Stevens. Eck said that John is as happy as a little boy with a new pair of red top boots with copper toes. This is not the first child for Mr. and Mrs. Stevens, though there are four girls, the youngest being seven years of age.

Two years later on December 18th, 1906 my grandparent's last child a baby girl named Ellen Cecilia was born at home on the farm at Canistota rounding out a family of five girls and one boy.

CHAPTER THIRTY-NINE

My grandparents did well on their Dakota farm with grandfather raising sheep, hogs and cattle. As Aunt Mae alluded to in her story grandma had her chickens that she excelled at raising. The price of wool was a dollar a pound in those years because there were no synthetic clothes available. A considerable amount of wool was sheared from each mature ewe every year resulting in an excellent source of income for the family. Grandfather also bought lambs locally that he fed out. He then shipped his finished lambs to Chicago by rail a distance of five hundred miles one way from Canistota. He always accompanied the sheep to market taking his six-shooter pistol with him that we still have in the family.

On occasion he would ride in the cab of the locomotive with his half brother George who was an engineer on the railroad. I remember seeing photos as a child in which several railcars carrying grandfather's sheep were involved in a derailment when the train hit a wash out on the rail line.

The Dakota snowstorms were notorious for their severity and duration. According to the history of McCook County Within These Borders the winter of 1888 was one of the worst on record with the temperature reaching -52F with much snow and wind. Both the Franz and Stevens's families would have had to endure that hard winter on their farms. After records started being kept the next worse winter was the 1968-69 winter season when eighty-three inches of snow fell.

Dad often spoke about grandfather having to tie a rope between the house and the barn to prevent him from getting disoriented in their raging winter blizzards. After coming to Alberta I am sure the family found our winters quite bearable.

Cousin Frank Collins recalled that the Stevens family had attended church services at Wellington. It was located about a mile and half east of their farm. Frank said the church had very high steeple that was plainly visible from the Stevens farm. Frank in his notes said that later the tall steeple became a hazard and the church was torn down. There was also a house at the site with a resident priest. After the demolition of the church the congregation attended services at St. Anne's Catholic Church at Humbolt that was about ten miles north of the old Wellington church site. The cemetery at Wellington is still in use.

CHAPTER FORTY

In 1902 grandma's brother John built my grandparents a new spacious story and half home on the high eastern section of their farm. Their home overlooked the western part of their farm with its scenic view of the Vermillion River Valley.

Among the few photo post cards that have survived through the years are several interesting ones from their years in Dakota. The first photo below shows the family standing in the yard on a summer day. It appears dad is standing in front of grandfather; he appears to be three or four years old. Grandma is seated holding I assume Aunt Ellen on her lap; to the far left I assume are two of the older Stevens girls. All that was written on the back of this old photo was J. D. Stevens farm home.

Among the items brought to Alberta by my grandparents was a huge twelve by fifteen-inch Atlas of McCook County. It included Spring Valley Township where their farm was located. It was more like an encyclopedia in that it contained a lot of United States and world history

It also had illustrations of business and farms located in the County. Under the Patrons Reference Directory they described the occupation and how long the individual had lived in the area. Beside grandfather's name they had John Stevens farmer, stock raiser, Spring Valley Post Office 1879, born in Wisconsin. Below is a photo of grandfather in front their home with several other members of the family standing in the front Veranda. The above photo was included with the Patrons Reference Directory of the Atlas.

RESIDENCE OF J. D. STEVENS.

They also listed Fr. B. Weber of Salem who had officiated at grandma's brother Ed Franz funeral services. In looking over the directory they always listed the year when a settler had first come to the area. There were perhaps three or four other individuals that had come to the area prior to 1879. In the article about grandfather when he passed on he was credited to have been one of the early settlers in the area. As I mentioned earlier we have to assume great grandmother and the family had moved from Minnesota to the farm at Canistota after great grandfather's Stevens passing in 1879.

CHAPTER FORTY-ONE

When grandma Joyce and I drove into my grandparents old farm yard in Dakota in 2002 we were very surprised to see their old farm house still standing. The survival of this century old home is a tribute to Uncle John Franz's excellent carpentry skills. It looked much like it did a hundred years ago when it was built in 1902. The yard was very neat and the whole place looked well cared for. Unfortunately there was no one home however after a series of phone calls I did finally locate a ninety three year old lady Marllys Erickson who had lived on the farm for fifty plus years.

70

She was now living on her own in a mobile home park in Sioux Falls. Her husband Albert had bought the farm in 1941 for twenty dollars an acre. When he passed away in 1982 she sold the west portion of the farm. They did not have any family so Marllys lived there alone for the next fifteen years. In 1997 she sold the remaining thirty-five acres and moved to Sioux Falls.

Marllys told me she had an interesting visitor on August 14th, 1958 who was visiting relatives at nearby Monroe, South Dakota. She was apparently from Texas and was a Doctor with the first name of Ann. She was very familiar with the house having told her she had been there many times as a young girl. The only possible relative I can think of would be a daughter of grandfather's half brother George. Doing these family histories sometimes provides more questions than answers regarding our family history.

She sent us pictures of the barns that have since been torn down. The windmill was still standing up on the hill south of the house when we were there minus the top blades. In the early days windmills were used as a source of power to pump water from farm wells. Another interesting fact she mentioned was that there was a big old barn down by the river when they bought the farm. I am guessing that is where the original Franz family home was also located. I assume grandfather wisely decided to relocate the building site up higher thus eliminating any possibility of the Vermillion River flooding the farmyard.

Marllys passed away at ninety-nine years of age shortly before Christmas 2007 after a short illness. Prior to her illness she was still living in her mobile home with some help from home care. Marllys is buried just up the road from the farm at the Wellington cemetery.

The new owners of the home have installed a basement, a deck on the north side and built an addition to the second level of the old house. My grandparent's old house is still standing at the head of Stevens Hill however it sounds like it has had an impressive makeover.

2002 Photo of Stevens' home built in 1902

**Looking west from the Farm Yard over original farm land
Old original Barn and windmill taken in 1950's**

CHAPTER FORTY-TWO

The next piece of the puzzle that would fall into place concerning my grandparent's eventual move to Alberta was a chance meeting of Nick Perrott and grandma's brother John in South Dakota in 1908.

Mr. Perrott had bought a section of land in Alberta in 1898 for three dollars an acre and was now planning to move his family there. He required the services of a good carpenter to help build his new Alberta farmstead. Mr. Perrott had been involved in farm real estate and the horse dealing business in South Dakota. He must have been favorably impressed with Uncle John's carpenter skills. The outcome of the meeting was that he agreed to help Mr. Perrott with the building of his farmstead. Uncle John no doubt silently thought that this would also be a good opportunity to check out that far away land where his father had passed away some eight years earlier.

On May 3rd of 1909 Uncle John Franz left for Alberta where he would live out his remaining years. Grandma Stevens saved an old post card he had sent from Sioux Falls, South Dakota to my grandparents at Canistota.

Front of the Postcard sent to my Grandparents with Sioux Falls the Brewery in the background

CHAPTER FORTY-THREE

After spending his summer in Alberta helping to build the Perrott farmstead Uncle John decided to establish an Alberta land base. On November 11th, 1909 he made an application for entry on a Homestead of one hundred sixty acres two miles west of Sandy Lake, N. E. of 32-55-1-W. On the application form he indicated he was a citizen of the U. S. and intended to become a British subject under the laws of Canada. The following requirements had to be satisfied before the applicant ever received the title to their land.

The applicant had to be over eighteen years of age and was required to put down a ten-dollar deposit. The second condition required the applicant to live on the land for six months every year for three years. The next and often what proved the most difficult task was breaking the required three and three-quarter acres of land every year for a period of three years. In many cases this required cutting the existing trees down. Removing the large tree stumps that remained followed this. The land was then broke as it was called with a breaking plow. The next onerous task was hand picking the many roots and rocks that remained. The following spring the land had to be planted to a grain crop. The last condition required two neighbors to sign an affidavit certifying the applicant had met their residency commitments. Alberta statistics for the early 1900's indicate that fifty four per cent of the applicants for homesteads were eventually successful in getting the hard won title to their one hundred sixty acres of land.

One of the neighbors who signed Uncle John's residency affidavit was my maternal great Uncle Patrick (Bud) Kinsella who was also homesteading in the area. His father Patrick Kinsella had come to the Riviere Qui Barre district to farm in 1902 from Pollock, South Dakota. The other neighbor who signed was Thomas Ellwood who with his family was living across the road from Uncle John's homestead land.

After Uncle John built a house and a barn on his homestead I assume he wrote to his brother Ed suggesting he visit him in Alberta. Annie Norris nee Ellwood writing in the Onoway History Book mentions that in 1912 their neighbors living across the road from them west of Sandy Lake were John and Eddy Franz. Several years later both the house and the barn on his Homestead were destroyed by prairie fire.

Uncle John had successfully completed all the requirements of proving up his Homestead except getting the required Naturalization papers. Unlike his sister Mary who never became a Canadian citizen Uncle John Franz had finally agreed to become perhaps a reluctant Naturalized Canadian citizen.

His Certification of Naturalization was issued on the 11th of March 1919. Slightly more than a month later on April 22nd a certificate of title in the name of John Jacob Franz was issued for his Sandy Lake Homestead.

CHAPTER FORTY-FOUR

Uncle John promoted the Alberta advantage with photo's of Alberta he sent back to Dakota prior to my grandparents coming to Alberta. This was perhaps his subtle way of indicating the unlimited potential that awaited them if they relocated to Alberta.

The first post card shows a photo of Qui Barre's main street taken in 1910 with the newly built St. Emmerence Catholic Church looming large on the right hand side. A group of stores and homes are shown on the left with Joe Paquette's store shown as the two-story building in the center of the photo. Uncle John wrote the following notation on the back. "This is the little town where I am now this is 9 miles from the rail head and 10 miles from my Homestead". The railhead he is referring to would be Morinville that then was the closest rail to Qui Barre. The distance from the railhead was a very important consideration in the early settlers mind. The railroad provided that vital link to the outside world for many of the otherwise isolated pioneer communities.

The next post card shows a group of men standing in what appears to be an excellent grain crop just before it is to be cut for harvesting. It looks like Uncle John is pictured fourth from the left with his trademark large black hat and dark suit coat. It looks like Ed Franz is pictured second from the right. He also wore a large black hat similar to Uncle John and was quite short. I am assuming the photo was taken on Sunday as they all appear to be relatively dressed up. My maternal grandfather Tom McNamara always kept his church clothes on for the whole day on Sunday, changing only to do chores. Uncle John wrote on the back of the post card "To Johnnie Stevens from Uncle John" there was no date written on the card however I would guess it was sent in 1913.

The last picture is of a group gathered for I assume a Sunday afternoon photo session. The photo may have been taken to document what appears to be an excellent crop of grain. To the left is a group of men with a team and wagon. I recognize Uncle Ed Franz who is standing and driving the team of horses with the wagon. It appears Uncle John is on the far right with his trademark black hat and dark suit coat.

In the good old Summer time

CHAPTER FORTY-FIVE

I thought it might be interesting to provide some background how the little
village of Riviere Qui Barre got its rather long French name. Long before

the first explorers traveled through what now is Alberta the Plains Cree called this general area of Alberta their home. Many of their descendants now live on a large tract of land located northwest of the village extending as far west as the eastern shores of Sandy Lake.

The village was named after a small creek which begins six miles north east of the village and meanders its way southwest eventually joining the Sturgeon River two miles west of the village of Calahoo. If you drive about two and half miles straight west of the village you will come to a little bridge that crosses the creek.

Apparently when the first white settlers arrived in the area the Cree had already named the creek "Kepoohatakaw" which translated means river that blocks the way. I presume the early residents of the district wished to have simpler and easier to pronounce name for the creek. An early French Settler came up with the idea of using the French translation of river that bars or Riviere Qui Barre for its new name. The name may be easier to pronounce however it is still a big handle for a small Alberta village.

Long before the village was established in the winter of 1823-24 Sir George Simpson of the Hudson Bay had a trail cut ninety miles to the northwest of Edmonton which passed about a half mile south of the village. It continued in a northwest direction eventually reached the Hudson Bay Fort at the present town of Fort Assiniboine. This early route was used to bring furs to Edmonton till about 1854. It was not used extensively again until the Klondike Gold Rush of 1898. A few hardy individuals were successful in completing the overland trail to it's terminus at Dawson City a distance of 1446 miles from Edmonton. Mom often spoke about as a young girl seeing the remaining wagon ruts of the old Klondike trail on their neighbor's farm south of the village.

The first post office was established two miles south of the present village in 1899. In 1902 it was moved north two miles with the village being officially surveyed in 1905 with street and avenue designations. In 1902 it was a thriving community having stores, blacksmith shops, drug store, creamery, hotels and a coal mine.

The village had high hopes of having a railroad come through the area however this was not to be. When the rail line passed through Morinville some ten miles north east of the village many businesses relocated there.

CHAPTER FORTY-SIX

Both Aunt Mae and Aunt Margaret remained in the United States when the family eventually came to Alberta. Fee indicated that his mother taught school in South Dakota before entering Nursing at St. Joseph's Hospital in St. Paul, Minnesota. She lived at home and rode horse back to the local school where she was teaching.

We have an old family photo of Voorhees Dormitory at Huron, South Dakota with the following notation on it. Miss Margaret A. Stevens, Huron, South Dakota, Voorhees Dormitory. From the information on the photo I would assume that Aunt Margaret went to normal school here prior to entering the teaching profession.

I recall dad mentioning that Aunt Mae had also taught school for a while south of Westlock. We are left to wonder where she went to Normal School however her old round trunk that survived for years in grandma's attic may provide some clues. It had a round Wells Fargo Emblem stamped on the top with Watertown, South Dakota label below. According to The South Dakota History Center at one time in the early 1900's Watertown had a large teachers College.

This excellent studio photograph below of the Stevens family was taken at Parker, South Dakota some time in 1912. I have never been able to locate another family photo with grandfather included.

Back Row starting on the left Aunt Kathryn, Aunt Mae, Aunt Margaret, and Aunt Irene. Front row dad, grandfather, grandma and Aunt Ellen.

CHAPTER FORTY-SEVEN

On January 8th, 1911 my grandparents oldest daughter Irene married a local farm boy Frank Fritz. After they were married Aunt Irene and Uncle Frank lived at Parker, South Dakota eventually coming to Alberta to farm when my grandparents emigrated.

On August 23rd, 1912 Uncle Frank and Aunt Irene's daughter Vera was born the first of my grandparent's eventual sixteen grandchildren. Sadly ten of the grandchildren were born after grandfather had passed on.

The photo below shows Dad and Aunt Ellen on the main street of Canistota in the early spring of 1913. They had come quite a distance from their farm that was ten miles south east of Canistota. They look sharp in their little buggy with the Shetland pony, I like Dad's hat. Dad was nine at the time with Aunt Ellen being seven years old. Both the Buggy and the Shetland pony would eventually accompany the family to Alberta.

Grandma wrote the following notation on the back of the photo June 15, 1913 from Johnny and Ellen. It was addressed to Mr. E. H. Franz, Monroe, S. D. who we would have to assume was visiting his sister Cecilia Miller and her family. Cousin Frank Collins indicated that the Millers farmed for years north east of the town of Monroe. It would be four years into the future before Ed Franz would go back to the Dakota's for the last time.

John and Ellen Stevens, Canistota, South Dakota Main Street 1913

CHAPTER FORTY-EIGHT

After I assume much soul searching my grandparents already in their mid forties made the decision to try their fortunes in far off Alberta, Canada. The Fritz family also decided to accompany the family on their long journey north.

My grandparents had worked hard to establish their Dakota farm for the past twenty-three years. Grandma's roots were even deeper having helped guide the farms fortunes since she was a teenager. I assume they still had the family adventurous spirit in their blood, as they both had been through relocations in their younger years. The glowing accounts of the opportunities that awaited them in Alberta reported by Uncle John Franz perhaps helped in their difficult decision.

Although I have no exact date when grandfather went to Alberta to select land for their new farm I would assume it was sometime during the summer of 1913. The chance meeting of Uncle John Franz and Mr. Nick Perrott in 1908 would continue to pay dividends for the Stevens family. Conveniently Mr. Perrott in addition to farming was now in the land assembly business for prospective new settlers to Alberta.

Grandfather selected three quarters sections of land in the Qui Barre district. The first one hundred sixty acres was four miles north of Qui Barre on the present highway #44. It was a relatively high land with a creek running through a small portion of the southeast corner. It perhaps reminded him of his farm in South Dakota which had the Vermillion River passing through it. The next property he selected was a half mile west; it had a fairly large home on it with some out buildings. This would be the new home of the Fritz family who had instructed grandfather to buy a farm for them in the same general area.

The last property he selected was one mile east of Qui Barre and three miles north a very high well drained high quarter. It had exceptionally well built twenty five year old log home on it. It had a similar construction design of buildings of that era that have been duplicated at the present site of Fort Edmonton. With his land selection process completed grandfather returned to South Dakota to prepare for the families eventual move north.

When coming to Alberta grandfather brought a copy of a letter of recommendation from his bank with him. According to the letter grandfather had been a customer of the First National Bank of Parker South Dakota for twenty-five years. The old original letter from the bank shown

84

below is quite faded. I have taken the liberty to print the original letter out on the computer. The wording in the letter seems very formal by today's standards. However at the time it no doubt was the correct form for a business letter.

To The Manager
Royal Bank of Canada,
Morinville, Alberta.

My Dear Sir: The bearer of this letter, whose signature appears below, has been a customer of this bank for the past twenty-five years, and we have always found him a desirable person to have on our rolls. He has always been prompt in his settlements, never exacting in his requirements, and a pleasant man to do business with. His relations with the community at large have been of the best, his credit unquestioned. We would bespeak of him, at your hands the best of accommodations.

CHAPTER FORTY-NINE

In March of 1914 the Stevens and Fritz families embarked on a twelve hundred and fifty mile train trip to establish a new life in Alberta.

They loaded most of their worldly possessions into rail cars, which included their Overland car, a full line of machinery, household goods, horses, chickens and their Shetland pony complete with harness and buggy. Grandfather and Uncle Frank traveled with the furniture, machinery and livestock with the rest of the family traveling in the passenger section of the train. As I referred to earlier Aunt Mae and Aunt Margaret did not join the families in their northward journey. Aunt Margaret was now completing her nursing studies at St. Joseph's in St. Paul, Minnesota. I would guess that Aunt Mae might have been teaching school in South Dakota.

I assume the family came north to Winnipeg then on to Edmonton, which would have been long train trip. Mr. Perrott greeted the family at the railroad station. They then were guests of the Perrott family until the home on the future Fritz farm was ready for occupancy. Aunt Ellen mentioned that it took them some time to get rid of the bed bugs that were then unwelcome residents of the house located on the new Fritz farm. All the railroad cars with livestock, machinery and furniture etc were shipped to Morinville for unloading.

CHAPTER FIFTY

My grandparents had left fully developed modern farmstead in Dakota. They were now faced with building another new home and farmstead in Alberta. The story and half home they constructed was almost identical to previous home in Dakota. They included many of the latest innovations in their new farm out buildings. The barn had a steel track installed just below the centre roofline that with a system of pulleys and a rope sling enabling hay to be lifted into the barn loft from a hayrack. They also had grain box that was lifted up similar to the hay sling. The oats was then placed into a bin that had been built in the southeast corner of the loft. The bin had an enclosed chute down to a box in the feed managers below. From there oats could be feed into the individual boxes located in each corner of the stalls.

Uncle John used a novel idea in constructing the hog house. It had a stairway to an upper level where the pigs slept. In all my travels I have seen very few of this type of hog barn construction.

A combination granary and cow barn was built south of the horse barn. The larger east section was used for grain storage and crushing grain for the pigs and cattle. The milk cows were kept on the west side of the building. A steel track was installed under the roofline similar to the barn and cables were attached to the same bin that was used for lifting oats into the barn loft.

Perhaps grandfather's most radical departure from local tradition was having a well drilled by a steam powered well drilling unit. The normal practice at the time was shallow hand dug wells with wood cribbing. Grandfather's well was one of the first drilled wells in the community. It was drilled to a depth of hundred feet where an excellent vein of water was encountered. A pump jack was installed and a gas engine was used to pump water.

In total they built fourteen different structures some very small and some very large. They converted the existing log home into a workshop. A blacksmith shop was added on the north side with a large storage lean too on the west side. There was a huge amount of manual labor required in the construction of these buildings. Considering all the lumber had to cut with handsaws before construction could even begin.

I am sure my grandparents and particularly Uncle John were well pleased with their summer building project. What once was practically a bare piece of prairie soil had been replaced with a new impressive farmstead.

CHAPTER FIFTY-ONE

An aerial photography company took the first aerial photo of the farm in 1952. I am assuming they took many photos of farms in the district and then came door-to-door selling the photos. They correctly assumed that many farmers would purchase the aerial photos when seeing the efforts of their labors viewed from the air. They were correct because over the years I have noticed a lot of these original aerial photos on display in local farm homes.

The aerial photo shows all the original buildings shown from the center to the top right of the photo. The building in the center with the green roof is old log house that was converted to a shop. To the right of it is the small garage grandfather had built for his Overland car. Their house is the large structure immediately to the right of the garage. Hidden in the trees is grandma's chicken house to the right of the house. To the left of it is the two-story hog house. Immediately to the left of it is the large horse barn. To the left and down the yard a ways was their combination granary and cow barn.

The house, barn and granary were all on concrete footings with large rocks mixed in with the concrete. The house had a small cellar under the front closed in porch.

On the far left hand side of the photo is my parent's home built in 1934. To the left was the chicken house that they had moved from the Fritz farm. Up the yard and to the left is the tall building dad had built for his first combine in 1940.

To the far left of the photo are the hundreds of trees that dad and mom got from the tree nursery in Indian Head Saskatchewan in 1945. My part in helping keep the trees alive was riding our horse Lightning while she pulled a stone boat with a barrel of water on it. Dad would than carefully water each little tree.

Aerial view of Stevens Farm taken in 1952 with many of the original buildings built in 1914 on the upper right

The photo following shows the somewhat stark appearing new Stevens home and yard in the fall of 1914 before grandma began her yard beautification work.

CHAPTER FIFTY-TWO

The family seemed to settle in to Alberta farm life very well. Perhaps the biggest event of 1915 was another member of the Stevens extended family arriving on the scene.

On June 15th 1915 Uncle Frank and Aunt Irene son Leonard Stevens Fritz was born. Leonard would be the second of my grandparent's eventual sixteen grandchildren. At the time Aunt Irene was not in the greatest of health as she was beginning to have problems with asthma. The doctors recommended that she move to a warmer and dryer climate. However in 1915 considering the challenges of finances and the long distance to a warmer climate this advice was much easier said than done.

The following photo's and stories indicate what life was like in the early days on the new Alberta Stevens farm.

We have an old photo from 1915 of grandfather's Oxen team on the road allowance in front of the farm. I would assume that they might have been included with the livestock shipped from South Dakota. As our earlier story about Mrs. Eastlick and her hardships indicated it was not uncommon for the early settlers to use Oxen. During the First World War there was severe shortage of work horses particularly in Western Canada. This resulted from thousands of horses being shipped to Europe to help in the Allied war effort.

The photo below has dad and Aunt Ellen seated happily on their wagon enjoying some Alberta spring sunshine immediately west of house in the yard. I assume the wagon was a product of Uncle John Franz's blacksmith and carpenter skills. A portion of grandma's well-fenced garden appears in the background. Woe to any animals either their own or the neighbors that attempted to gain access to grandma's prized garden. The lower level of the chicken house is also shown in the background of the photo. Rising chickens and gardening was a labor of love for grandma.

The above photo was in the form of a post card. It was addressed to Margaret Stevens, St. Joseph's Hospital, St. Paul, Minnesota. As I mentioned previously Aunt Margaret was in training there and would later graduate in

Nursing from St. Joseph's in 1918. Grandma wrote on the part reserved for a message on the back of the post card "John and Ellen 1916".

The photo below was taken while Aunt Margaret was in training at St. Joseph's Hospital. Aunt Margaret is on the left with a nursing associate to her right.

The photo following in the form of a post card has dad seated on their Shetland pony. It is obvious he has just returned from a successful hunting trip with some prairie chickens and a bush rabbit. The note on the back written to Aunt Ellen by dad indicates that going to church and hunting were two activities that dad enjoyed doing on Sundays.

In the early years there was excellent fishing at Sandy Lake that I am sure was an enjoyable pass time. In addition fish provided a much needed change from the farmer's red meat diet. The undated family fishing expedition photo below has Uncle Ed Franz, grandfather, Uncle John and several other unidentified persons showing off their catch of Jackfish.

They appear to standing on a section of pier that was installed to access the new Ferry that been installed at Sandy lake in 1914. It was built to cross a narrow section of the Lake with two larger sections of the Lake on either side. Unfortunately the Ferry operated for only three years until 1917.

A new ferry was put into service in 1921 and operated till 1929. The above information was taken from a book entitled Ferries and Ferryman in Alberta published in 1986. The book was among the possessions of your paternal great grandmother Nora Stevens when she passed on. She is listed among the contributors to the book.

Left to right Uncle Ed Franz, grandfather, unknown, Uncle John Franz and unknown

In the this yard photo following taken later in the summer of 1916, grandma was well on her way in developing her prized yard featuring flowers and a excellent producing garden. In later years grandma would plant three apple trees in this section of her garden. In the background the barn is pictured on the far left. Shown to the immediate right is the pump house that was built to cover their newly drilled well. Shown on the far right is Uncle John's one story and half hog house.

CHAPTER FIFTY-THREE

In settling into their new surroundings I am sure the family experienced many cultural adjustments with new neighbors, school, church and the community. The farm home was where neighbors frequently gathering to visit and socialize. According to Aunt Ellen's recollections during the First World War the Red Cross held sewing bees at farm homes in the district. During the meetings the ladies would sew articles of clothing for soldiers who had been wounded and were now hospitalized.

Perhaps the first major social event on every farm where the farmer had built a new large barn was having a barn dance in the loft of the barn. This usually happened shortly after completion of the barn or in the fall before any hay or straw was stored in it. I can recall the smooth floorboards of the barn loft which no doubt made an excellent dance floor. Our neighbor Joe

Falls mentioned to me all the good-looking Stevens girls that were in attendance at the Stevens barn christening.

The 1947 photo below although years ahead in our story content I think best exemplified Uncle John's high building standards. After thirty some years the barn is still standing tall and proud looking I assume much like it was when newly built in 1914. The small metal sign with the year 1914 on it is visible directly underneath the large upper barn door. Yours truly is shown astride Lighting the only remaining work horse left on the Stevens farm. Lighting must have been given her name for a reason however all the years of fieldwork had mellowed her disposition considerably.

To the left and in the background is their faithful stock trailer built by Uncle John years earlier. The trailer would remain in service until 1952 when dad bought the first truck on the Stevens farm a used two-ton Dodge.

I really like the photo of grandfather shown following looking quite pleased with his traveling rig. He appears to be headed out somewhere with his horse and buggy. By the looks of the leather seats it was a top of line model. The caption on the top of the photo reads "Democrat" buggy. This was the most reliable method of summer transportation for many years even after the arrival of the first cars.

Interestingly when I was in grade one in 1941 we often went to Belle Valley School with our neighbor Lewis Falls using similar transportation.

CHAPTER FIFTY-FOUR

No family history would be complete without including stories about the local one room schoolhouse. The local school district had been named Belle Valley when it was formed in 1901. The school was located a mile and half northwest of the Stevens farm. Before community halls were built many social functions were held in the local schoolhouse. Among the many activities were Christmas concerts, community dances, meetings and even the occasional wedding dance. According to The Wheels History Book their little one room school was replaced with a much larger school in 1920 with grandfather being secretary treasurer of the then Belle Valley School district.

The following information is from The Wheels of Time History Book from an official document obtained from the Department of Education. It was requested by our old neighbor Gertie (Sheehan) Campbell on the origins of our local Belle Valley School.

"According to our records the Belle Valley School district No. 626 was established on August 23 1901. Authorization was given on September 29, 1920 to borrow the sum of eight hundred dollars for the purpose of building a new two-room frame schoolhouse, with concrete basement and foundation and purchasing furnace and two acres of land for a school ground. Mr. J. D. Stevens was Secretary-Treasurer". Sadly no names were available as to who the first individuals were that had the foresight to organize the Belle Valley School district in1901.

I am not aware of how many wedding dances were held at the Belle Valley School. I do however recall mom telling me about Dick and Maggie Wills's wedding dance that was held in February of 1934 at the school. The school property was surrounded by the Wills farmland that made them very much local school district residents.

Mom's most poignant memory of the evening was how the bride's brother Roy Johnson managed to stand all evening while providing a marathon session of great violin music.

Our good friend Allen McDonnell recalled recently how a group of his neighbors including Uncle Angus and Aunt Ellen McGillis had made the twenty mile round trip with a team and sleigh to attend the Wills wedding dance. Allen said the Wills family insisted that they put their team of horses in the Wills horse barn while they attended the dance.

Aunt Ellen recalled attending her first ever dance at the Belle Valley School. The first dance for the evening was a square dance and her partner was our confirmed bachelor neighbor Dan Falls.

An old neighbor Vic Douziech told another interesting school story to me. Apparently when he and his brother Nap started school at Belle Valley they could only speak French. During the day they became increasingly frustrated with this strange sounding English language. During an afternoon recess break they decided they had enough of this English school. Taking matters into their own hands they ran back to their farm which was a mile and half away. Noticing their absence the teacher sent two of the older students Dad and Rene Bourbonnais to the Douziech farm to get them. Some eighty-five years later Vic still laughs when he recalls how he and his brother were rather reluctantly brought back to school by dad and Rene.

The undated early photo following shows a group of students with the Belle Valley School in the background. There is an x mark above two students in the back row. I think Aunt Ellen is third from the left and dad is toward the end of the back row. I would assume that Belle Valley School was where Dad developed his skills in baseball, competitive running and high jumping. The inscription on the back reads Belle Valley School with members of the Boddez, Borle, Bourbonnais, Fitzgerald, Norbert, Sheehan, and Stevens families included in the photo.

According to dad's recollections there was sometimes a problem which bell was ringing at Belle Valley School. Was it the teachers hand held bell that summoned the students in from recess or the sound of a much larger bell located very close to the school? In the next chapter I will relate the interesting story of the Willie Wills family and their dinner bell.

CHAPTER FIFTY-FIVE

My grandparent's immediate neighbors to the north were the Willie Wills family whose land I previously indicated surrounded the Belle Valley School. Many of our early family summer photos included visiting members of the Wills family. Dad often mentioned Willie's illustrious past and how being well passed fifty years of age he began a new farming venture in Alberta. I am also indebted to Maggie Wills who included their family history in The Wheels of Time History Book.

Their Alberta story begins very similar to the Stevens family in that Willie ran into Mr. Perrott somewhere in western Canada on a train during his search for a new land base for the family. The result of this meeting was that the Wills family put down roots in the Qui Barre area in 1910.

Similar to both my paternal great grandmothers Willie had Irish roots beginning life in Mayo County Ireland where his parents were tenant farmers. Willie had little use for the English sheriffs who raised the rent ever time the tenant farmers got a head. They refused to sell the land to the tenant farmers even considering the Wills family had English origins.

As a young teenager Willie left to work in the Glasgow shipyards eventually setting sail for the United States. Arriving in Pennsylvania he worked in the coalmines becoming an expert in handling explosives. His next move was to a rocky farm in Wisconsin where he used his dynamite skills in helping clear the land of large rocks. He also became proficient in drilling water wells into the stony formations of neighbors land.

Willie got tired of fighting with his rocky farmland. As we alluded to earlier Willie had looked far afield for better land. In 1910 the family left Wisconsin with carloads of machinery, livestock and household items destined to be unloaded at Morinville, Alberta.

Among the many items the family brought with them was a bell from an old train locomotive. Willie being the innovative type installed a high pole beside their farmhouse on which he hung the locomotive bell. It was used to call the men in from the fields at mealtime. Dad often mentioned what a novelty their dinner bell was in the local community. It could even be heard plainly ringing at the Stevens farm located about a half mile across the field to the southeast from the Wills farm.

Some years later a bad summer storm blew the bell down from the steeple at our local St. Emmerence church. The Wills family came to the rescue and graciously donated their dinner bell to the church. As a young boy one of my vivid memories of attending church was the former Wills dinner bell ringing loudly announcing the beginning of ten o'clock Sunday morning services.

CHAPTER FIFTY-SIX

Across Alberta the early pioneers erected hundreds churches with many denominations being represented. In many communities a small hall was built close to the church where social functions were held.

After their arrival in the district St. Emmerence Catholic Church at Qui Barre became an integral part of the Stevens family with them attending weekly Sunday Mass there. They also participated in the annual church picnic and other fund raising activities. Both dad and mom played many ball games at the church picnic that was held for years on the second Sunday in June.

The church had been built in 1902 on land donated by my maternal great grandfather John McNamara. My maternal grandfather Tom McNamara assisted in hauling the lumber for the new church. It measured ninety-six feet long and forty-eight wide with a square footage of over four thousand feet. It was an ambitious project for a small community with the church being officially blessed by Bishop Legal of St. Albert on November 16th, 1902.

In a recent conversation with Aunt Ellen she indicated that Bishop Emile Legal at St. Emmerence confirmed dad and her in the spring of 1916. She also remembers that a group of men rode out with horses to greet the arrival of the Bishop before Mass. According to her that was a custom routinely practiced in those early years when the Bishop came to a parish for an important occasion.

The photo shown below, I assume, was taken at home after the Confirmation Service. Both Aunt Ellen and dad look very well groomed for their important day. Aunt Ellen also indicated grandma was an excellent seamstress and no doubt had made Aunt Ellen's confirmation dress. She also remembered how grandma had huge cutting scissors and would cut out four patterns at a time when making dresses for the older girls in the family. Their Overland car is shown on the far right indicating it was the mode of travel used by the family to attend the Confirmation service that spring morning.

Aunt Kathryn, Aunt Ellen, grandfather, Dad and Aunt Margaret

St. Emmerence Church in the 1950's

Another story revolving around Sunday services at our local parish was told to me by Mrs. Victor (nee Kramps) when well into her nineties. She recalled how their family sat behind the tall Stevens family during Sunday mass. She also remembered seeing dad riding the family Shetland pony with his long legs dangling by his side. The photo above shows St. Emmerence church still looking great after fifty plus years of service to the community.

CHAPTER FIFTY-SEVEN

Even in Alberta's formative years politics was a topic that captured the interest of most rural people. The following stories and photos are an example of how these issues were debated and eventually passed in law.

An organization called the Temperance and Moral Reform Society was formed in Alberta and across Canada in 1907. Its purpose was to promote the complete ban of all liquor sales except for medical purposes. The local drug stores in essence would become the only outlet allowed to sell alcoholic beverages. The local doctor would then become the final authority on who received a prescription to buy alcoholic spirits. By 1914 the Society to abolish all consumption of alcohol had five hundred canvassers out in Alberta.

On July 21st of 1914 a vote was held with the results in Alberta being 58,295 for and 37,509 opposed. The results were similar right across Canada; it was now official no more public sales of liquor in any establishments except drug stores.

Interestingly the voters of the St. Albert constituency voted against the imposition of prohibition with 666 opposed and 307 in favor. At the time a large rural area north of St. Albert was included as part of the St. Albert constituency. No doubt my maternal great grandfather John McNamara who was owner of the Shamrock Hotel at Qui Barre had opposed the legislation. In many cases this legislation was the death knoll for many small country hotels.

Politics at the local level was never too far from people's mind even on Sundays. It was not uncommon after Sunday mass during a provincial election to have political meetings in the local parish hall. Aspiring politicians running for office would speak to the parishioners after mass, talk about a captive audience. In later years I recall Lucien Maynard who was then the Attorney General in Ernest Manning Social Credit Cabinet speaking to us after church in the parish hall.

The following story was told to me by my maternal grandmother Elizabeth McNamara about a local politician named Lucien Boudreau. As was the custom on Sunday during an election campaign he spoke to the parishioners after church services. Apparently Mr. Boudreau was very short in stature and during his speech someone from the audience said, "Mr. Boudreau you should stand up" to which he replied, "I am stand up"

He was a member of the Provincial Legislature representing the Liberal party for St. Albert and the farm area to the north. The big issue at the time was Women's Franchise whether ladies should have the right to vote. Mr. Boudreau was opposed to giving ladies the right to vote.

He made the two following statements in the Legislature, "The place of women was in the home" and "Women would do the best they could for its welfare without meddling in the public affairs of the province." Unbelievably he won his seat for another term.

The provincial Legislature did approve the right for ladies to vote in 1916; however the new United Farmers of Alberta party defeated the Liberals in 1921. Since their defeat in 1921 the liberal party has had a long drought not managing to get elected for the past eighty-seven years in Alberta.

Michael Hogan and Lucien Boudreau

CHAPTER FIFTY-NINE

Four years after coming to Alberta in the spring of 1917 my grandparents bought one hundred and sixty acres two miles north of their home farm from Mr. John Lutz for twelve hundred dollars. This land became known as the north place as long as we owned it. It had many wet areas some of which were surrounded by trees that were home to a lot of wild life. There was also a huge slough immediately to the south and east of the quarter. This area formed part of the headwaters or beginnings of Riviere Qui Barre River. With the purchase of this land my grandparents were now farming a section of land that was considered a large farm by 1917 standards.

Their first project on their new land was building a barn on the south east corner of the quarter not too far from the road. Uncle John built the barn that held eight horses; it also had a small loft for hay storage. The barn was a great labor saver in that the horses could be kept there over night eliminating the two mile trip home in the evening and return trip back in the morning before field work began. Grandfather fenced the land and brought the cattle up in the spring after seeding was completed. The grass adjoining the wet areas made excellent spring pasture. The grass surrounding the sloughs was cut in late July or August for winter feed for the livestock. It was cut using a horse drawn mower, raked into coils and let dry. It was then stacked using a team and hayrack, later to be hauled home with a team and sleigh in the winter.

CHAPTER SIXTY

In 1917 grandfather was elected to the Morinville local board of United Grain Growers shareholders. Unknown to grandfather at the time a member of our family would sit on the local U. G. G. board for the next seventy plus years.

At the time the local board had worked hard selling the sufficient numbers of shares to allow a UGG elevator to be built at Morinville. The fledging company had been formed in Manitoba in 1906 by a group of farmers in attempt to obtain a better price for their grain crops in the market place. In 1919 grandfather was elected secretary of the local board a position he held till he passed away in 1925.

Below is a copy of the minutes in grandfather's handwriting of a special meeting of the U.G.G. local board held at Morinville, February 18th, 1919. From reading the minutes we would have to conclude that the Elevator was not open twelve months of the year. Secondly the shareholders were in unanimous agreement the elevator should be operating all year. Their efforts were successful and Company agreed to their request. As we can appreciate it took a lot of effort to obtain what later was routine policy of having all grain elevators open for business twelve months a year.

In looking over the old frayed records of the minute book of the UGG local their problems did not end with keeping the Elevator on a yearly basis. At another meeting of the U.G.G. local held November 15th, 1919, the following request was in a copy of their minutes. "A resolution that a road should be made so that we can get at the elevator at any time in the year." Access to the elevator which in later years was taken for granted apparently was not a given in the early years of U.G.G. The fledgling UGG local established in 1917 held three more meetings in 1919.

Meeting of the Morinville Local
#131 of the United Grain Growers
held at Morinville on Jan 6th 1919
The meeting was called to order by
Mr. E. Rivet the chairman. Members of the
Board present. E. Rivet. Chm. Geo. Halley —
John Schaffer. J. D. Stevens. Members
Absent. Emery Bellier.
Minutes of the last meeting was read &
approved. the report of F. D. McRae as
Delegate at the Convention held in Calgary
on Dec 18th 1918. was well delivered.
also the financial statement ending aug. 31st
1918. all the share holders that was not
at this meeting have missed a very instruc
ive meeting, as Mr. McRae gave a very
good account of the Convention.
the See was instructed to write to Calgary
& try & have the Elevator here open the full
year. & why the Elevator can not buy grain
or contract with the farmers for his grain
before it is hauled, as the line Elevators is
doing.
                    Adjourned to meet in
Morinville at 2. P. M. on Feb 1st
1919.

                    J. D. Stevens
                              See.

110

Meeting of the Morinville Local #131 of the United Grain Growers, held at Morinville on Feb 18th, 1919 at 4.30 P.M.

Members of the Board present. E. Rivet, John Schaffer, Geo. Hawley, E. Tellier, J.D. Stevens.

The meeting was called to order by the Chm. The reason for calling this meeting was to see about trying to have the Co. keep the Elevator open. At this meeting there three representatives of the Co., Mr. W. A. Warr special representative of the Organization Department and T. J. Martin of the Elevator Dept., and G. Campbell of the Livestock Dept. The question of keeping the elevator open was taken up and the secretary was instructed to write to the Co. at Calgary and tell them that it was the unanimous vote of the meeting to keeping the Elevator open. It was estimated at this meeting that half of the 1918 crop is yet to come to market.

J. D. Stevens
Sec.

Morinville, April 10th, 1919

The transfer of share 3114485 to 114486 from Adelard Riopel to Charles Riopel. The above transfer was sent to Calgary on above date.

J. D. Stevens

The correct address of the following
Hubert Saux
Geo. Bouchard
Walter Moser
History of UGG in Morinville

The photo following of the UGG elevators in Morinville was taken in the 1970's. Gillespie Grain Company built the small old elevator in the centre in 1908. A lot of the elevators built prior to 1900 in Western Canada had a similar design.

The elevator below would be where grandfather would have first hauled his grain by team and wagon or sleigh after coming to Alberta. On a cold winter day the sixteen-mile round trip would have been a challenging journey. Unfortunately we do not have any photos of the 1917 elevator built by U.G.G. in Morinville however I assume it would have been adjacent to the old Gillespie elevator.

111

After much soul searching apparently from lack of business the UGG structure in Morinville was dismantled and rebuilt it at Mearns in 1928. UGG would not have another elevator in Morinville until 1943 when they purchased all the Gillespie grain elevators in Alberta.

The big new elevator we see on the right in the above photo was constructed in 1958. However thirty plus years later a huge Inland Grain Terminal was built west of Morinville by UGG. Its presence in part is due to the determination and foresight of grandfather and the other early UGG local board members in their resolve to keep a company presence in the area against many odds.

Footnote
The oldest remaining grain elevator in Western Canada is located at Fleming Saskatchewan. It was built in 1895 by the Lake of the Woods Milling Company. It is of very similar design to the Gillespie elevator in the above photo. A photo of Fleming elevator was featured on the back of Canadian dollar bill in the early 1950's. Interestingly instead of the normal engine power, the Fleming, Saskatchewan elevator's leg was initially powered by two horses on a turn belt.

CHAPTER SIXTY-ONE

From viewing old family photos it appears that grandfather was interested in other community activities besides the U. G. G. and the local school board. I really like the photo below that was in Aunt Ellen's photo Album showing the then mayor of St. Albert Michael Hogan and grandfather. They appear to be engaged in a serious conversation no doubt about some local problem. By the background it looks like they are up on Mission Hill where Father Lacombe first established a mission in 1861. It is a very scenic location overlooking St. Albert and the Sturgeon River Valley.

My maternal grandfather Tom McNamara often mentioned Mr. Hogan in his conversations however grandpa always called him Hogan. Grandpa was a Municipal Councilor during the twenties for the M. D. of Ray. His total salary for 1930 was one hundred and eighty dollars and forty cents, which included his mileage. He hired local farmers to maintain the roads in those early years. Interestingly perhaps as a forerunner to official bilingualism in Canada their municipal financial statement for 1930 was printed in both English and French.

Mr. Hogan was then their secretary treasurer and the majority of Council meetings were held in St. Albert. Hogan Road on the west side of St. Albert is named after him in recognition of the contribution he made to St. Albert in its formative years.

CHAPTER SIXTY-TWO

In early 1917 grandma's brother Ed Franz went back to St. Paul, Minnesota. As we mentioned in chapter thirty Aunt Margaret was nursing there and Ed hoped to get help for his worsening health problems. Unfortunately they could not help him and he passed away on his return trip home.

Grandma saved the following obituary notice that I assume was in a Canistota newspaper describing his passing while on a snowbound train in Minnesota.

Mrs. Harry Collins (Who was my grandma's youngest sister Alice) received word Sunday that her brother Ed Franz had passed away. Ed had been at St. Paul taking treatment for kidney and heart trouble. The doctors finally told him that his home physician could do all for him that they could and so with his niece, Miss Margaret Stevens, who was in St. Paul with him, started for home.

At Windom, Minnesota they were snow bound and Mr. Franz died on the train at that place. Miss Stevens continued with the body of her Uncle to Salem. Harry Collins went to Salem Monday to make arrangements for the funeral. Miss Stevens came home with Harry Monday noon, all going to Salem Tuesday morning to attend the funeral that was held in the Catholic Church that afternoon. Rev Fr. Webber, who happened to be on the train when Ed died, preached the funeral sermon. Interment was made in the Catholic cemetery, beside the body of his mother who had gone before him.

Great Uncle Ed was fifty-one years old at the time of his passing. Being the oldest of the family he had seen a lot of hardship in his life with the loss of four siblings. It was not an easy fate in those early days to be disabled when hard physical labor was required for most jobs.

Uncle Ed's physical limitations did not stop him from joining the family and later his brother John on their journeys of discovery to new places and new lands. I am sure he thought he had lived a good and interesting life. According to Aunt Ellen Ed had driven delivery wagons back home in Dakota. The good Lord was good to him in that Aunt Margaret Otterson was with him during his final hours on the train. As the obituary notice of Ed's passing indicated he was laid to rest beside his mother in St. Mary's Catholic Church cemetery located west of Salem. Below is photo of Ed Franz the notation on the back reads Ed Franz 1915. Cousin Frank Collins also wrote the following note on the back. "Who took this, when or where I have no idea?"

In the summer of 1917 the Fritz family also decided to leave Alberta in search of a warm drier climate better suited to Aunt Irene's health. Not really sure of their final destination they set out on their long journey south. When they reached Raton, New Mexico, which was just over the border from Texas, they decided to put down roots. Uncle Frank found employment with the Santa Fee Railroad with Aunt Irene's health gradually improving.

Vera, Aunt Irene, Leonard and Uncle Frank

CHAPTER SIXTY-THREE

On June 19[th,] 1918 Grandfather officially joined the ranks of the Alberta cattle fraternity when he applied for and received his own personal brand letters. His cattle could be now officially identified with the brand S7 with a half diamond above the S7 that was placed on the right hip of the animal. He no doubt thought that this was necessary because he was now pasturing cattle on the north place away from the home quarter.

Any cattle that were lost or stolen could easily be identified by their brand. The cattle were branded with a long iron bar that was called a branding iron with the designated letters and numbers on the end opposite the handle. The branding iron was placed in hot coals and then placed on the desired location of the animal that was to be branded. There was a central registry that carried all the records of all brands in Alberta. All registered brand owners paid a fee that in 1918 was three dollars and fifty cents for four-year

116

term. We still have grandfather's original branding iron in addition to an electric one we had made in later years.

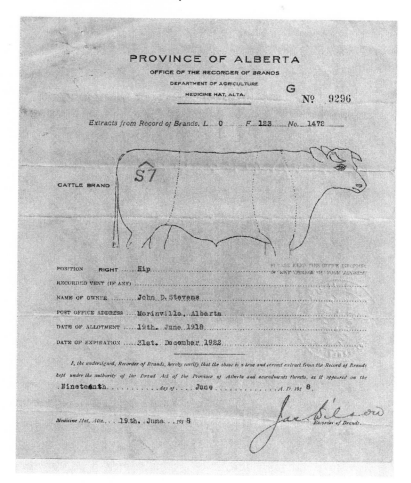

In 1992 the Calgary Stampede and Exhibition Board invited our family to attend the seventy fifth anniversary of grandfather's brand registration which was held in conjunction with the 1992 Stampede.

All the cattlemen who still had ownership of their original brands registered in 1918 were invited to attend. It was a class program with free tickets for the rodeo and other functions. They also presented our family with an attractive cowhide banner. Our brand, grandfather's name and date of brand registration were engraved in the center. The hair on the hide indicates that the hide was taken from a Shorthorn cow. Grandfather had raised Shorthorns when he first came to Alberta, a fitting tribute to his cattle selection of long ago.

Pictured following is an early photo of grandfather's blue shorthorn cow with a halter on. The straw shed that grandfather built to protect the cattle from the wind and cold is shown in the background.

THE "BLUE COW"

CHAPTER SIXTY-FOUR

When the Fritz family headed out with no specific destination site in mind it no doubt greatly concerned by grandparents. The fact that they had found an ideal location suited to Aunt Irene's health must have given them some consolation. However in the early summer of 1918 my grandparents made a decision that grandma should make the long trip to New Mexico to check out the health of their oldest daughter Irene and her family.

To grandma's credit she saved the letters that grandfather had wrote to her while she was away visiting in New Mexico in 1918. Upon grandma's passing I assume Aunt Kathryn in her wisdom kept them. Cousin Myra Morin thankfully made the same decision when looking over her mother's keepsakes. Andy and Myra graciously gave copies of them to me. I guess we could consider them a three generational Stevens chain letter. From the date of grandfather's first letter to grandma we would have to assume that grandma left Alberta in late June of 1918 on her long train trip south.

I took the liberty of printing grandfather's old letters off on the computer. One has to wonder if grandfather's formal education ended at age twelve with the sudden passing of his father in 1879. I recall my maternal grandfather Tom McNamara lamenting about what little formal education he had received in his youth. Grandpa had gone to a one room country school in Kansas in the mid 1880's. It was only during a few winter months of the year that he had the opportunity to attend school. During the remaining school year work at home on the farm took precedence over grandpa's educational needs. I would assume that grandfather Stevens also was faced similar circumstances after the passing of his father.

Below is the hand written copy of grandfather's first letter to grandma written on July 5th, 1918.

Morinville Alta. July 5th/1916

Dear Mamie, we got your letter today that you wrote in Denver, & the one you sent from Nebraska a day or so ago my but you had a slow ride. the next time take the sleeper suppose is is a little higher you dont go so much, & think you can take a sleeper. but do that any more & get all tired out, it might make a person sick & then that would be worse, we expect to get a letter from you on monday. telling us how you got there & how Irene & Frank & the Kiddies are, I expect by this time. that Vera & Leonard is having a good time with Grand Ma. we are getting along fine, it rained every day this week but Monday & today wednesday it rained all day & yesterday it only rained a Hard Shower at noon so we did not loose any time today was nice & the grain is sure growing some. I think in another week that the wheat will be Headed out it is starting to shoot in the head now, Ellen is going to write some too so she will tell you the news if there is any. Now I want you to take better care of yourself than you did on the road down, Love to all
            your Loving Husband, J.S. Stevens

121

Morinville Alta, July 5th, 1918.

Dear Mamie,
We got your letter today that you wrote in Denver and the one you sent from Nebraska a day or so ago. My but you had a slow ride. The next time take the sleeper, suppose it is a little high. You don't go so much and think you can take a sleeper. Don't do that any more and get all tied out. It might make a person sick and that would be worse.

We expect to get a letter from you Monday telling us how you got there and how Irene and Frank and the Kiddies are. I expect by this time that Vera and Leonard is having a good time with grandma.

We are getting along fine. It rained every day this week but Monday and today. Wednesday it rained all day and yesterday it only rained a hard shower at noon. So we did not lose any time. Today was nice and the grain is sure growing some. I think in another week the wheat will be headed out. It is starting to show in the head now.

Ellen is going to write some too. So she will tell you the news if there is any. Now I want you to take better care of yourself than you did on the road down. Love to all. Your loving husband, J. D. Stevens

Morinville Alta, July 12th 1918.

Well Mamie how are you and all the folks down there. We are getting along fine up here. We got your letter and Irene's letter you wrote when you got down there. Oh yes there was quite a large space here after you left. It seemed as more than one was gone. But now since we heard from you down there and you got through and is with Irene we are feeling fine.

Now Mamie don't be in a hurry to come back for we are all right. I feel as though your visit with Irene will help her. As you know it is better than medicine sometimes. I expect the children are having a good time with you by this time.

Mike Wills was over here the other night and came through our field from the northwest. He said he never seen a better crop then we have. The wheat is heading out and everything is good. Last night it rained again but the weather is warm. It is the best it has been since we came here. The timothy is in first blossom now it will be the earliest it has been yet. Harvest will be earlier than ever.

Our wheat on the north place is fine too. I have John Bailey here with his tractor breaking. After next week I think that we start disking so to get it done before haying. JJF is going to help me through harvest. I told him he might just as well because it paid just as good as carpenter work. He offered to help so he won't take any carpenter work through harvest.

Joe Falls and Tommy Welch both go to Edmonton today for examination. Tommy says he looks to be sent to Calgary. He has reported twice.

That spotted cow with horns on is milking and that red heifer. The heifer is over in the pasture yet. We are going to get her home someday and see how she is for milking. The children are writing too so they will be telling you the news. Alex McGillis is exempted to Nov 1st , we seen it in the Bulletin.

Now try and enjoy yourself and make it pleasant for Irene. The children are just as good as they can be. Will close with love to all. Your loving husband, J. D. Stevens

Morinville Alta, July 26th 1918.
My dear wife.

Well how are you and the kids getting along. I suppose that Frank is gone by this time. We are all fine up here.

Mae came home Tuesday morning and packed her trunk and went again in the afternoon. She has gone to Unity Sask. She has got in the Grand Trunk railway service. Is a night operator with over a $100 a month. She was in the office at Edmonton for a week before they sent her down there. She is all taken up with her work.

Yes I sent our Lodge dues to Canistota. Sam Morrow and the children came up Sunday and went back Monday. Mrs. Morrow went to Canistota. She took Jimmy and the twins with her. Sam did not go any where else while he was here, went straight back home again. We had a good visit, they all sure enjoyed it.

Graham's has got a Ford car. Woods is worse than ever. Mr. Wood has left home and is in Edmonton. If it was me some of them boys would go. It is to bad for Mr. Wood. Sam says he is too good to them.

The crops around Millet are not so good as up here. It has been to dry down there. We had plenty of rain here.

We had a frost Tuesday night. It killed the beans and scorched the tops of the potatoes some. People differ in opinion about the wheat being hurt some. I think in the low places it is hurt some. I don't think our wheat here at home is hurt. But up on the north place on the north side down towards the slough in places I think it is hurt.
We have not heard from N. Dakota yet but look for it every day. By your last letter we got a week ago today you intend to stay until in Sept. Did you think twice when you wrote that? See it is nearly the first of August. It will be by the time you get this letter. So you see that Sept is not far away.

Did you get the draft we sent you. I will send you the other one next week so you will have it.

Can Irene run the car or have you got some one of the neighbors that will give you and Irene and kids a ride. We haven't run our car much since you left. We aint got time.

Well Mamie the children are all asleep yet. I guess I will call them up now. I have been going to write in the evening but the last two evenings we had company. Mr. Elwood and last night Pat and Mary was over. So I got up and writing this the first thing. It was a week ago today that we sent you that draft in the last letter.

The children are all going to write so they will tell you the rest of the news. Will close for this time. I hope that you and Irene and kids are enjoying yourselves and that your visit will do Irene good.

Love to all. From your loving husband, J. D. Stevens

After Breakfast so will write a few more lines. I am breaking yet, I have got a nice lot broke. Bailey only broke 10 ¼ acres. His father came down so he had to go home. Mr. Fitzgerald can not get any one to break for him. Pat said last night that they offered Meunier $8.00 per acre to break but aint got time. Pat and Frank are both over here. They are breaking but they wanted to get a lot broke. They will soon have to go haying.

The weather is nice and warm again. It was cold for a few days wore my Mackinaw in the field. I only summer fallowed part of the land. I was going to where I hauled on manure. I have got a good crop of barley. If I had of disked that land we would have had a good crop on all of it. W. Young is breaking for Wills now. They did not break a bit themselves.

Morinville Alta, July 28th 1918

Well my dear Wife and children.

We received your letter yesterday telling of your nice ride up the mountains. That letter we was looking for from N. Dak. was laying over in Morinville. You see we have a new Post Master. She did not send us any notice. So Kathryn went over Friday and called for J.J.F. mail. There was a registered letter laying there for him. They would not let Kathryn have it. So she told them to send it to Qui Barre. So John went down and got it today.

The check is for $90.00. You can see on the check what it is for the interest to July 7th 1918 on contract for purchase N.W. ¼ 6-144-67. It was drawed to John alone so he had it made payable to you. You can get this cashed now to leave your money in the Bank until you need it. Now Mamie if you think you will need any more write. As for you to need money coming home at the line. You will be all right as you are coming home and as your register card will show. They can't keep you out of here if you had not any money. So if you want to buy anything don't be afraid about that.

We got a letter from Mae today telling us of her work. They are good to her there in the depot. She likes her work. I suppose you will have a letter from her by this time. Mae said in her letter that she was going to write to you and Irene. It looks as though Kathryn had a letter not go down but she is satisfied whatever was you think.

You bet Kathryn gave us plenty to eat. I was telling her yesterday that her butter was so good and you know she makes good bread. Then last night we got your letter saying that you could smell the butter soon as you answered it. It is to bad we could not send you some butter. Kathryn is doing fine cooking.

By the way I heard that frost of last Tuesday night was bad in some places. McLeod had 150 acres of wheat he is cutting it and the minister Mr. Kelley was hit hard to. Norman right north of them is nice and green. It is to bad for them as they was both hailed out last year and froze out this year. They say McLeod feels pretty bad about it .

I think we wrote all the news Friday that was the day before yesterday but I want to send you this money so you will have it. Now get this cashed as soon as you get it. You see it is a cashiers check it is alright. But you know that is the proper way to do. Love to all. Your Loving husband J. D. Stevens

CHAPTER SIXTY-FIVE

In the following chapter I will attempt to enlarge on some of the topics grandfather was discussing in his long ago letters to grandma.

Although grandfather had no way of knowing how world events would eventually unfold 1918 was a pivotal year in Canadian and world history. Later that year in October the worldwide flu pandemic would began its deadly march across Canada. A month later on November 11th Armistice was declared effectively ending hostilities in World War One.

However grandfather's main concern at the time was grandma's welfare and the health of his daughter Irene and her family. He also gave grandma his assurance that the children were doing well in her absence. He also referred to Aunt Kathryn's excellent cooking especially her butter and bread making skills that apparently were very much appreciated by the family. I particularly liked his reference to grandma being away from the family when he wrote, "there was quite a large space after you left". In the following paragraphs I will attempt to further elaborate on references to people and events that grandfather mentioned in his letters to grandma.

The J.J.F. that grandfather mentions were the initials of Uncle John Franz. After my grandparents came to Alberta Uncle John moved off his homestead and made his home with them.

Grandfather seemed pleased in his letter of July 26th that Aunt Mae had got a position as a night telegraph operator with the Grand Trunk Railroad at Unity Saskatchewan at one hundred dollars a month. A year later on July 28th 1919 Aunt Mae married Bert Kirwan a dispatcher with the Grand Trunk Railroad. Grandfather mentioned that Aunt Mae had packed up her trunk before leaving for her new position with the railroad. As we referred to earlier Aunt Mae's well-traveled old trunk was stored for years up in grandma's attic with its well-worn wooden slats on its exterior.

In a recent conversation with Cousin Jack Kirwan he recalled how his parents when attending a movie sometimes used their expertise in Morse code to communicate with each other. Using Morse code they would pass touch signals back and forth with their legs that of course the other movie patrons were totally unaware off.

Grandfather always included the weather, crop conditions and the progress of ongoing farm work to grandma in his letters. In his letter of July 26th, 1918 to grandma he wrote a simple short sentence regarding a heavy frost that occurred on the previous Tuesday evening. Sadly at the time grandfather did not realize the devastating effects that Tuesday night frost would have on the outcome of the farms crop yields that year.

To put a more meaningful perspective on the above described events I did some research in an old book of dad's entitled Furrows, Faith and Fellowship by Norman F. Priestley and Edward B. Swindlehurst published in 1967. The information I obtained was surprising and sad.

I will quote from the book "On the morning of the 24th of July, a heavy frost struck the central parts of Alberta. As much as eighteen degrees below freezing were registered, completely killing all the wheat, leaving only worthless straw." The writers went on to say, "Not a threshing outfit moved that season". The authors continued, "Some oats and barley grew into good green feed, which sold toward the spring of 1919 at prices so high that men slaughtered cattle they fed through one of the longest winters on record rather than buy more feed."

In order to help the war effort Alberta farmers had been urged to plant more wheat in the spring of 1918. Unbelievably Alberta farmers responded by planting an additional million acres of wheat in the spring of 1918. This dramatic increase in acreage really impressed the book's authors. Doubly so considering a Federal government Order in Council of April 21st, 1918 called all young men aged twenty to twenty two years of age to report for military service. This government Order essentially removed many young farm men from the Alberta farm workforce. Grandfather talks about neighbors Joe Falls and Tommy Welsh going to Edmonton for examination in one of his letters to grandma.

The authors included a graph showing how devastating this frost was on yields of Alberta grain crops in the fall of 1918. Considering there was an extra million acres of crop seeded in 1918 the yields were dismal six bushels per acre as compared to eighteen bushels an acre the previous year. Weather conditions were sometimes cruel to the fortunes of Alberta farmers.

In his letter of July 26th to grandma he indicated that a neighbor a Mr. Elwood had come to visit one evening. The Ellwoods had previously lived across the road from Uncle John Franz at Sandy Lake. They moved to a farm a mile and half northeast of my grandparents in the spring of 1918. When visiting with Elsie the youngest of the Ellwood family about five years ago she recalled her father going over to the Stevens farm to buy some feed grain from grandfather. Elsie was eight years old at the time of their visit to the Stevens farm. Some ninety plus years later she fondly recalled grandma's hospitality in inviting them in and serving them cake.

Elsie is now ninety-nine years young and does exceptional well considering her age. Like many of the early settlers the Elwood family had their share struggles in adjusting to Alberta farm life. The Elwood's had emigrated from England in 1910 and their first home was on a quarter section rented from Mr. Perrott a mile north of Qui Barre.

In the Calahoo Trails history book Annie their oldest daughter relates an interesting incident that happened to the family while they were living on the Perrott farm. "One fine evening in the spring of 1910 my parents called us children outside to listen to "some happy neighbors having a party laughing their heads off" only to find out later we had been listening to coyotes.

Another of Elsie's recollections was how the family after leaving their farm close to my grandparents rented my great grandfather John McNamara's farm at Qui Barre in 1921. Great grandfather had passed away in 1919 and his Shamrock Hotel was now vacant. The family used part of the Hotel as their principal residence with them using the former Hotel saloon area as what we would describe now days as a recreational room. The family would on occasion hold a dance for family friends in the old saloon area.

On a personal note when I began selling real estate one of my first customers was Annie's sister Mary Walker (Ellwood). Mary had a parcel of land east of Calahoo with a for sale by owner posted on it. I was successful in convincing her to list it and sell it through our Company. Probably the best part of the sale as far as Mary was concerned was the traditional meal I had with my clients on the completion of the sale. I invited Mom and Aunt Margaret Fitzgerald along who did a lot of reminiscing with their good friend Mary about happenings of years gone by.

Grandfather mentions Sam Morrow and some of his family coming for what he described as "a good visit they all sure enjoyed it." Dad said the family would go down occasionally to visit the Morrow family at Millet. Being curious of what had become of the family I eventually contacted Sam's grandson who is named after his grandfather.

He still is living in the house his grandfather built in 1915 when the family came from South Dakota. Interestingly the Morrow's immediate neighbors in South Dakota were grandma's sister Alice and her husband Harry Collins. An update on the Morrow children who were visitors at the Stevens home that long ago July 1918 proved interesting. Vera the oldest girl ended up living on an acreage in the center of the present city of Victoria. Sam said his Aunt pastured eight Angus cows there for years. She also ran a campground on her property. In lieu of paying camping Fees on occasion the campers would help out in keeping the campgrounds clean. This life obviously agreed with her because she passed away this past November at one hundred and five years of age.

In speaking with Myra recently she said her mother often mentioned the Morrow family and particularly Vera the oldest girl. In 1975 Aunt Kathryn and Aunt Ellen had the opportunity to go to Victoria and reconnect with Vera after not seeing her for fifty plus years.

As for the rest of the Morrow family, Bob ended up taking medicine and practiced for years in Lansing, Michigan. One of the twins which grandfather mentioned went back to South Dakota and farmed on his Dad's land close to Canistota. Jimmy took over his dad's farm at Millet where his grandson Sam is now living.

Sam said his grandfather had come to South Dakota from a well-established farm in Ontario. Besides farming he also taught school in South Dakota. When he came to Alberta he would occasionally officiate at Sunday services at a local Wetaskiwin church.

In his letter of July 28th grandfather mentions that Uncle John Franz had received a check for ninety dollars from North Dakota in lieu of interest charges on a land purchase of N W 6-144-67. As grandma's brother Ed had passed on the previous year was it possible that he had owned this unidentified parcel of land? The fact that Ed may have owned land in North Dakota perhaps could be described as our family's best-kept secret. The challenge I now faced was locating the above-described property in vast land area of North Dakota. Who did I still know in North Dakota who still was in the land of the living?

The Western Producer farm paper that I mentioned in the introduction had a regular contributing writer Ryan Talyor who owned a ranch at Toner, North Dakota. Having read his columns for years I felt comfortable in contacting him with my request. After having a discussion on the merits of raising Angus cattle I inquired about the location of what grandfather referred to as 6-144-7. He indicated it had to be somewhere about sixty miles south of their ranch.

On checking the map I called Jamestown, North Dakota for the number of the County Recorder. Having searched for many titles in the U.S. in the past I knew this was the starting point in our investigative process. They were very obliging and located a Homestead title in Stutsman County registered in Ed's name.

They sent us the above Homestead receipt from June 17th, 1908 indicating he had paid the balance of seven dollars and five cents required by law for entry of N.W. 6 -144-67 containing 140.99 acres. In 1917 after nine years Ed still was the registered owner of the land. The next question we would have to ask ourselves is how did he ever manage to prove it up with his limited ability to do manual labor? One possible answer is that he had the necessary capital to hire others to do the hard work for him. The land in question may have been all grassland that would have made breaking the land a lot easier.

According to their County map Ed's homestead had no sloughs on it and very productive farmland. The County land records indicated that the family received forty five hundred dollars from the sale of Ed's estate. I am sure Ed would have been pleased with the excellent return on his very small initial land investment. We would have to ask ourselves another question why did Ed select this area of North Dakota to file for a homestead? The paragraph below may provide us a possible answer.

In 2004 LaVerle Stevens from Sioux Falls, South Dakota sent me photos and information on the Donovan and Stevens's family. Among the photos was one of great grandfather John Stevens in his later years that is included in the book.

She also sent a photo of the children of Mary and Thomas Donovan, Thomas was a brother to great grandmother Ann Stevens. In the letter she mentions that they were first cousins to Lucy Smith (Grandfather's sister half sister.). In it she also indicated that the Adam Smith family (Lucy) had lived in a sod house between 1898 and 1900 in Stutsman County North Dakota. I assume grandfather and Lucy kept in touch so she may have suggested that grandma's brother Ed select land in that area for his new homestead.

In his July 28th letter to grandma grandfather mentions "McLeod" being froze out. This of course was the frost on the Tuesday night of July 24th that grandfather referred to in one of his letters to Grandma. As Mr. McLeod had served as a casket bearer at Uncle John Franz services I wondered what our connection to the McLeod family was. I assumed that Uncle John had done some carpentry work for the McLeod family.

Interestingly on doing further research I found out that Uncle John had indeed built both the McLeod's home and their large horse barn. Dianne McLeod a widow who was married to Mr. McLeod grandson Rod is still living in their original farm home. When I recently phoned Dianne and inquired about some history on their farm buildings. Without hesitation she

132

proudly told me that John Franz had built both their home and their big horse barn that is also still standing. The big barn was built to replace a barn that had been destroyed by fire. To my knowledge the new barn that replaced it was perhaps the largest barn that Uncle John built in the area. The old eighty plus year old barn is pictured below still standing tall and proud against the elements.

To conclude our discussion of grandfather's letters we have several old photos that have survived taken while grandma was on vacation in New Mexico. The photo below has grandma all decked out in a fancy traveling suit with matching hat. One wonders if grandma had made the suit as part of her traveling wardrobe. Aunt Mae in recounting her childhood family memories made the following quote about grandma's sewing skills. "Mother was a fine seamstress and made every stitch we wore"

133

The photo shown below of Aunt Irene was also taken while grandma was down visiting the Fritz family. Her coat looks as though it is the very latest in fashion design with her hat style very similar to the one that grandma is wearing.

CHAPTER SIXTY-SIX

In 1919 grandfather obtained an Overland Agency that allowed him to sell cars from the farm. The fact that grandfather had owned an Overland car before coming to Alberta perhaps helped in his being awarded this sub dealership. Aunt Ellen had a group photo shown below of Overland car dealers which included grandfather. I assume that it was taken in Edmonton in what appears to be the announcement of their new 1919 Overland. She passed it on to her grandson Larry McGillis with a negative of this old group photo. Amazingly this excellent group photo was developed from the eighty plus year old negative. We also have on old Alberta license that belonged to grandfather that has the letters Dealer on it. Grandfather's health problems began in 1923 that I assume ended his association with the Overland Company.

I never asked Dad about grandfather's involvement with Overland Company and he never really discussed it. Herman Kieser of Morinville related an interesting story about one of grandfather's car buyers to me. Herman remembered that when his dad would drive his new Overland car to Edmonton he always covered it up with a canvass while there. Owning a car was considered a privilege in those early days and they were looked after with kid gloves so to speak.

The following background information on how the name of the Overland car evolved is courtesy of the Stan Reynolds Museum in Wetaskiwin. The name Overland was decided over a coffee break during the fall of 1902 by Charles Minshall president of Standard Wheel Company of Terre Haute, Indiana and Claude E. Cox. Cox had just graduated from the Ross Polytechnic Institute in Chicago. Cox's thesis involved a project in which he had devised a four-wheel car out of a motorized tricycle. They began production of their car however unfortunately a few years later they ran into serious financial problems with their car-manufacturing venture.

A buggy manufacturer named Parry rescued them and offered to back production of their new car. John Willys, whose Company later developed the famous Jeep, arrived on the scene and put in an order for five hundred cars. As luck would have it a serious economic downturn occurred. Parry cancelled production and lost his investment including his home in 1907.

Willys took over the company and started up production of the Overland in 1909. He manufactured forty nine hundred cars with a six cylinder forty-five horsepower engine. In October of 1917 they came out with a new model that featured a self-starter and headlights. Production was scheduled for one hundred and forty thousand cars. They challenged the Model T Ford car cost wise with a price tag of less than five hundred dollars. We would have to assume that this was the model that grandfather was selling in 1919. The following comment by Msgr. Walter Fitzgerald was in the Wheels of Time History book regarding one of the sales techniques that grandfather used to sell Overland cars. "John Stevens Sr. had an agency for Overland, a real fancy car with a roll back top. He used to take prospective buyers for a ride and show them how the Overland could climb the St. Albert Hill and pass the poor little old Fords that had to shift to a low gear".

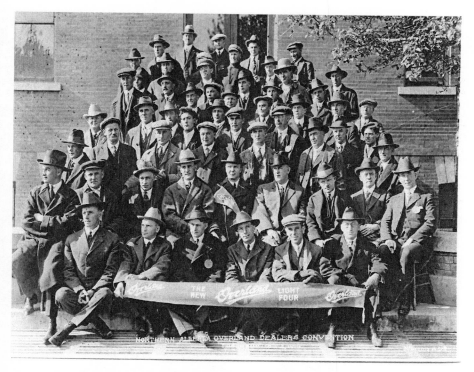

Grandfather pictured at Edmonton Overland sales meeting. He is in the 4th row second from the left

John D. & Mary Stevens 1918

Grandfather and dad with the top down on their Overland car. I like
the angle of their hats.

THE OVERLAND CARS

SIMPLICITY and certainty—these are two vitally desirable qualities in an Automobile.

Power, comfort and elegance are desirable; essential, even; moderate cost combined with efficiency a virtue; speed and ability factors; but today, *simplicity* is the thing—simplicity with certainty.

An Automobile is, after all, only a conveyance—the most modern way of quickly and comfortably getting where you want to go. Incidentally it may be a great source of pleasure; primarily it is a practical convenience. Its speed has been demonstrated; its power, comfort and ability shown: motor cars in expert hands are daily accomplishing the impossible;—all this is common knowledge,—and yet, among all the cars there are, how many possess the element of simplicity?

Take the one question of control. Ordinarily this is complexity itself. There are foot-levers, speed-shifts, gears to mesh; the disengaging of the clutch requires strength; gear-shifting is an art; constant judgment is required; to get in a wrong gear may wreck the car. Often there are complications on both sides and in front, all demanding attention and contributing something to the task of getting the car there and back. It is strange that with the wonderful development of the industry so little attention has been paid to simplifying the car,—to combining power, speed, and unfailing ability in a mechanism so automatic that a child could operate it. The question naturally arises —"Is there not, today, *one* such car?"

Assuredly there is. It is shown and described in the following pages; a car so good as to be adopted by the United States Postal Service, so desirable that for years our factories have not been able to keep pace with orders, so plain and sure that even a timid woman can confidently drive it anywhere.

Examine it piecemeal and you will find instance after instance where a single effective device has replaced many complicated parts.

One such innovation this season did away with no less than sixty-five individual pieces. All forgings, castings and other supporting fixtures are so modeled as to do several duties at once. Intricacies are avoided; ingenuity is at a premium; simplicity is insisted upon. This is not merely good designing; it is good sense. Instead of being a car for an expert to tinker with, the Overland is built for the average person to run.

Consider its simplicity of control—literally as easy as walking. You put one foot forward to go ahead, to the rear for reverse. The high speed only requires a push forward with the other foot on another pedal. That is all there is to it. Either pedal disengages the other. It is impossible to get in two speeds at once, or to inadvertantly get into reverse. Even if a mistake is made and the car is started on "high," it can do no harm.

Three of the 1910 Overland Models have "only pedals to push." The driver cannot go wrong, cannot strip his gears, cannot injure his car by an error in judgment. The fourth Overland Model, equipped with Selective Sliding Gear Transmission, is practically as simple. The Clutch is so perfectly balanced that it can be disengaged by a push of one finger, and yet it can never slip. The gear shifts slide easily, change without burring, and operate noiselessly. The whole car is a delight to an expert, and a pleasure to the novice.

Overland cars have so repeatedly demonstrated their staunchness, ability and unfailing readiness that it seems needless to emphasize these qualities here. The United States Government employs them daily in the Postal Service, private owners are using them for every imaginable purpose over all kinds of roads throughout the country. They have been repeatedly tested out on long endurance runs, used as Official Cars in public contests, driven from coast to coast by novices, and even, in several cases, by women, and yet there has never been a complaint. The experience of Overland owners is most conclusive evidence of merit.

Prices range from $1000 to $1500, depending on the model chosen. These are extraordinary figures for a good car, but the price is an incident rather than an argument. It is due to the very simplicity of the car itself, and to the remarkable facilities possessed by its builders. It requires no argument to show that 20,000 cars can be built at lower proportionate expense than can 2,000. But far more important than its low initial cost is the Overland's saving of operating expense, its economical upkeep, and its freedom from necessity of repair.

You are invited to test for yourself this wonderfully simple and efficient Overland Car.

To conclude our discussion of Overland cars I think the above photo is very appropriate. It has grandma Joyce pictured beside a restored 1911 Overland car similar to grandfather's first car. The car is proudly on display in the entrance area of main building of the Alberta Reynolds museum at Wetaskiwin. Stan Reynolds took it in trade many years ago and wisely added it to his prized antique car collection. This display assures that the Overland car that contributed to Alberta's early automobile history will be available for future generations to admire.

John Steving, Frank / Ellen Steven

CHAPTER SIXTY-SEVEN

No family history would be complete without discussing the difficulties the family encountered when they ventured forth with their car on the early country roads. Rain in the summer combined with snow and extreme cold in the winter often added to the challenges the early travelers faced. The undated family photo above I think captures the spirit of our topic. It appears from the photo that Uncle John and Aunt Ellen are all decked out in their finery and are headed out in their Overland car. Dad has his work clothes on and may or may not have been accompanying them on their road trip. He is wearing his favorite farm work attire, his blue bib Overalls. They would remain dad's trademark working clothes for the rest of his farming days.

Aunt Ellen recalls less than ideal early country road conditions in The Wheels of Time history book with a story entitled "The Corduroy Road"

The car did not get any use in the wintertime but was jacked up and put on blocks until spring. The road south to the main road usually had a mud hole until a long spell of dry weather had come to pass, but with the help of "corduroy" the process was speeded up. Corduroy is a series of poles laid across the mud hole until there is a solid bottom and not too much mud above it. A couple of "pushers" in the back seat was a help but it was a "dirty" deal if one got caught directly behind the rear wheels while in the act of "pushing".

A trip to Edmonton was something to get ready for. Morinville was one milestone to accomplish, but there was a piece of slough land two miles south of town that often proved a challenge to the driver and the horsepower of the car. After that on to St. Albert and the hill south of that community was an effort, but coming home the one north of it was longer and steeper. A sigh of relief when home was in sight.

The photo below has grandfather stopped and repairing a flat tire on their Overland car. According to Aunt Ellen flat tires were a frequent occurrence on the early model cars. It appears that grandma and Aunt Ellen are catching up with their reading wearing their very designer hats. It is possible dad may be pictured on the far right with only his large foot wear in plain view.

Aunt Ellen continues her story about the challenges the family faced on the road while traveling to the city. "Tires did not last long and there was usually a flat with a trip of that magnitude. A spare was always in shape but if two flats occurred, there was the task of patching a tube and having cement and plenty of patching material along. After that, pumping up the tire and hoping the patch held. After a muddy spell there were two ruts in the road. When that set got a bit deep another set was started, straddling the first two. That was when the driver had to make a decision as to which to take. If he got stuck he knew he hit the wrong pair of ruts".

The following story was told to me by cousin Ron McGillivray of his harrowing experience many years ago when returning from a summer trip to the city with dad. The main road between Edmonton and Morinville had improved considerably from the road conditions Aunt Ellen described in her above story. However the rural side roads sometimes still presented a huge driving challenge. A sudden rainstorm could quickly turn a dusty country road surface into a slippery wet driving nightmare.

Dad and Ron had gone to Edmonton to pick up some summer-hired help. While they were in Edmonton apparently dark storm clouds rolled in from the northwest. This was a signal to them that they might face challenging road conditions on their return journey home. The first part of their trip home was uneventful until they turned west off the relative safety of the gravel highway that ended at Morinville. They were now faced with eight miles of slippery wet road before they could reach the relative safety of the Stevens farmyard. The absence of deep ditches on the early country roads was a blessing in disguise. One of the perquisites of navigating a muddy country road was maintaining a fast enough speed to prevent the mud from rolling up into huge globs on the cars wheels. However the faster you drove the less control you had on the direction the car was headed. To Ron's amazement he remembered how dad spent as much time driving in the ditches as he did on the road. With dad's excellent driving skills and more than a little luck they eventually did get back home to the Stevens farm.

Cousin Donna Paschal Ron's younger sister has her own memories of the challenges muddy summer roads sometimes presented on their trips out to the farm to visit grandma. The time frame had to be the early 1940's and by

145

this time there was gravel of sorts on the main seven-mile road west of Morinville. The problems however began with the mile of dirt road that honestly was up hill all the way to the farm. Maybe grandfather having lived on Stevens Hill in South Dakota preferred an Alberta farm located on similar high ground.

Donna's story starts when Uncle Mac and the family left the relative safety of the Morinville road and ventured north towards the Stevens farm. Uncle Mac had a very cautious approach to life in general. I would assume this tendency also carried over to his operation of his motor vehicle. Uncle Mac's driving motto was perhaps don't speed and you will arrive safely. As we discussed earlier when driving on a muddy roads the person operating the vehicle on occasion had to throw caution to the wind and drive fast. According to Donna Uncle Mac's passengers urged him to speed up on the muddy Stevens road however his natural inclination was to slow down. Donna did not indicate if Uncle Mac took the advice of his back seat drivers and threw caution to the wind. I would guess that the issue of what was the proper speed for driving on the sometimes muddy Stevens uphill road was never completely resolved.

Aunt Ellen in her story of their driving experiences in the early years on the farm indicated their car was parked most of the winter months. However as the years progressed the family car saw limited use during the winter season. Driving conditions in the snow however could be much more challenging then attempting to navigate a muddy road in the summer. Driving fast on snow bound road was no guarantee of safe passage through the oncoming snowdrifts. Often country roads became impassable to automobile traffic after a winter blizzard.

Cousin Ron McGillivray related the following story of how dad used his ingenuity in getting help out to grandma's during her bout with pneumonia in the late winter of 1932. Normally Uncle Mac would bring Aunt Kathryn and Aunt Margaret out with his car to help care for grandma. In the time frame we are discussing there were no such things as regular snow removal from country roads. The problem that confronted Uncle Mac that particular weekend was the seven-mile east west road from Morinville to our south corner was impassable as the result of a recent snowstorm. It ran seven miles west connecting to the one mile of road up to the farm. To overcome the snow-blocked roads dad enlisted the help of some kind hearted farm neighbors to the east. Many lived along that seven mile stretch of snow bound road. At one-mile intervals a farmer with a team of horses and a sleigh would exchange my aunts who were passengers in their sleighs. This kindly exchange between neighbors continued until I assume dad did the final exchange at our south corner one mile from the farm. This coordinated effort by kindhearted neighbors enabled the girls as grandma affectionately referred to my Aunts as to safely reach the farm where their help was needed with grandma's care.

The photo following was taken some years later; however by the looks of the car snow clogged roads were still a huge challenge. Perhaps mom took the picture to celebrate us arriving home safely. This big black car with the protruding hood reminds me somewhat of the automobiles members of the Royal family used in their motorcades in years past.

On a more serious note dad had purchased the car a 1935 Master Delux Chevrolet from Louis Tremblay who had a G. M. dealership in Morinville. The subjects in the photo include dad seated on the car fender with yours truly sitting on his knee. It appears my little dog Rex also is very happy that we were back home.

Although the following story told to me by cousin Ron McGillivray is not directly related to the challenges of navigating wet or snow bound country roads. It does however indicate that even when the roads were quite passable mechanical car problems would often leave travelers stranded awaiting help.

Ron did not indicate what year his dad purchased their car however it was manufactured from 1909 to 1940 by the Hupp Motor Company of Detroit Michigan. According to Ron most of their engine problems often happened on their return trip from the farm back to the city. By the time Uncle Mac had got to Morinville he often became quite aware that the engine in his Hupp car was not performing as it should. Ron indicated that their engine problems originated with the car's vacuum pump. As we referred to earlier Louis Tremblay had a large garage and G. M. dealership located on the main street on the west side of Morinville. However often they did not have the required expertise to deal with Uncle Mac's engine problems. This necessitated placing a call to the city for help from a mechanic at the Edmonton Hupp dealership. Ron indicated that sometimes the wait got very long indeed before the Hupp mechanic came to their rescue with the necessary parts to get them started again on their journey home.

I thought the late 1948 winter photo following depicts how the wind could pile snowdrifts up on country roads. By 1948 the local municipality made attempts to keep the country roads open in the winter months. However their efforts caused ridges on the roads that in many cases helped the snow to accumulate even more on the roads. In the photo below a Caterpillar tractor with a blade attached to the front had gone through creating a very narrow opening for single lane traffic only. Mom and I are shown in the photo below with our 1948 Chev car in the background.

As our above stories indicate on occasion car travel on country roads was sometimes not possible. Mom wrote the following notation on the back of this early 1940's photo shown following. "Johnny returning from Sunday Mass roads impassable." This then was the reason for dad resorting to the most reliable method of transportation on the farm our horse Lightning. Who could safely travel the eight mile round trip to Sunday morning mass regardless of the road conditions. It would be at least fifteen years into the future before we would have the luxury of having gravel roads for our Sunday morning car trip to church.

149

This 1952 summer photo shown following was among dad's keepsakes from his many years as a director of U. G. G. I think it is fitting conclusion to our topic of car travel on our early country roads. It reaffirms that in Alberta's formative years Mother Nature could wreck havoc with the best-made travel plans. The exact location of this section of muddy road was not given however it was up somewhere in the vast Peace River Region. The occasion was a summer tour by the Board of Directors of United Grain Growers of their grain elevators located in the Peace River Country.

As we can appreciate from most of the above stories and photos our admirable present day Alberta road system had very humble beginnings indeed.

CHAPTER SIXTY-EIGHT

Farm mechanization arrived on the Stevens farm in 1917 with grandfather's purchase of a new three wheel red 10-20 Case tractor. The photo below has their new Case tractor in the field while the operator appears to be taking a break from plowing. By the look of all the family members gathered around the tractor it was obviously a novelty on the Stevens farm. It is difficult to envision that at the time this tractor represented the latest in modern farm technology. It appears from the photo that it required considerable amount of ingenuity to attach the one bottom plow to the rear of the tractor.

From left to Right: Unknown, Unknown, grandfather, Unknown, Aunt Irene with Vera on her lap and Aunt Ellen holding her doll.

The 1917 fall harvest scene below has grandfather posing for the photographer while taking a break from operating the new Case tractor as it powers the threshing machine. Their trusted Collie dog is apparently also impressed with the new iron horse on the Stevens farm.

The photo following has dad as a lankly teenager proudly standing beside the Case tractor while taking a break from fieldwork.

John y Steven
1916
Case Tractor
Power - 10. 20

CHAPTER SIXTY-NINE

In the early twentieth century the majority of farm young people's education ended when they completed grade eight. Both your great grandmothers Nora Stevens and Annie Goulet did not have an opportunity to go beyond grade eight in school. A lot of the girls if not needed at home to help worked as hired girls for neighboring farm families. The fortunate few would go on to Nursing, Business school or to Normal school to become teachers.

Our local school Belle Valley did offer grade eleven in those early years. However in recent conversation with Aunt Ellen she said the teacher a Miss McDonald just taught for the very bright kids and paid no attention to the others. She said dad was having difficulty in some subjects. When she related what was happening to my grandparents the decision was made that dad and Aunt Ellen would attend high school in Morinville the following year.

The result was that in 1921 they attended the Morinville Convent for their grade eleven. Aunt Ellen must have skipped several grades because they were both in the same grade. They drove the Overland car in the spring and fall which in itself must have been quite a challenge considering the condition of the roads.

In the winter months they boarded at the home of Mr. and Mrs. August Krauskopf. August owned the local Blacksmith shop and John Deere dealership in Morinville. Aunt Ellen recalled how her bedroom was located directly above dad's on the main floor. Upon awaking in the morning she would take a broom and bang on the bedroom floor alerting her brother John it was time to get up and get ready for school.

Both Dad and Aunt Ellen contacted chicken pox during the school year and were absent from classes for many days. The result was that they both failed grade eleven which Aunt Ellen told me just recently was the only grade she had ever failed. Aunt Ellen went on to attend MacTavish Business College however she had to discontinue her studies when grandfather began having health problems. Fortunately in later years she did complete her course at MacTavish. As we indicated earlier in our story farm work both in the house and outside had to often take priority over the educational needs of the family members.

The 1921 photo below shows Aunt Ellen, dad and Aunt Margaret all decked out in their best Sunday attire. The caption on the back reads Ellen, John and Margaret Stevens. On the back of the photo K. Stevens was written with the year 1921 under it obviously the photo belonged to Aunt Kathryn.

CHAPTER SEVENTY

In 1922 two more sons in laws joined the extended Stevens family. On August 9th, 1922 Aunt Margaret married Edward Otterson in Edmonton. According to cousin Fee Otterson his parents had first met at a summer picnic at St. Albert.

The following year on August 6th Aunt Kathryn married Alexander McGillivray in Edmonton.

The summer photo below was taken at picnic at St. Albert in 1921 with Aunt Kathryn seated on the far left, next to her is Aunt Margaret and Aunt Ellen is seated to her right with the white hat. In the center Uncle Eddie Otterson is shown wearing a cap. Uncle Mac McGillivray is kneeling on the far right.

In the undated harvest scene following Uncle John is shown to the left with grandfather to the right next to their team of horses. It looks like dad is on the far right holding I assume a shot gun with I think Uncle Mac McGillivray to dad's left. Again I assume the photo was taken on Sunday as everyone except grandfather appears in his or her Sunday best. Uncle John has his overalls covering up his suit pants. Ducks and upland birds were very plentiful in those years. Even if a person took a casual walk to inspect the crop you often took the shotgun along. By the height of the stooks there appeared to have been a bumper crop of oats on the Stevens farm that year.

CHAPTER SEVENTY-ONE

In 1923 grandfather began experiencing numbness in his legs. Although he consulted local Doctors they could not diagnosis the problem and it continued to get progressively worse.

In the late winter of 1924 my grandparents must have made the difficult decision to go to the Mayo Clinic in Rochester, Minnesota to seek a second opinion on grandfather's leg problems. Dad mentioned that grandfather had attended grade school with two of the sons of the founder of the Mayo Clinic. The Mayo family like the Stevens family had deep roots in Rochester.

The founder of the Mayo clinic Dr. William Mayo had served at Rochester during the Civil War. He stayed on after the war ended eventually establishing a medical practice there. It became known as the Mayo Clinic in 1915 with his two sons taking over the practice. As the years progressed the clinic acquired an outstanding reputation in treatment and diagnosis of difficult medical cases.

I would have to assume the expenses of traveling, doctor's fees and the possibility of grandfather being hospitalized weighed heavily on my grandparents' minds. After looking at all their options they must have decided to have a farm sale in the spring of 1924. This I assume was done to assist in the funding of their upcoming travel and medical expenses. Selling most of their worldly possessions except their land would not have been an easy decision for them. Watching these items, which in many cases have taken years to accumulate, being scattering to the winds on sale day would not have been easy.

According to dad grandfather had a very strong aversion to paying interest charges. So raising the necessary cash by having a sale although difficult eliminated the thought of paying some banker interest charges later.

We note from reading at the sale bill that Edmonton was still very much rural oriented city in 1924 with Ball's Stock Yards located a block and half north of the down town Post Office. The free lunch advertised on a spring farm sale day always attracted more lookers than buyers. However that being said a farm sale was and still is a time when rural people meet for food and fellowship.

A copy of their March 12th, 1924 sale bill is shown following.

AUCTION SALE

In Morinville District

Mr. J. D. Stevens

Owing to poor health has rented his farm and is leaving the District. He has instructed the undersigned Auctioneers to sell at Public Auction on his farm, being

Southeast Quarter Sec. 8, Tp. 56, Rge. 26, West 4th

Located 7 miles west and 1 mile north of Morinville, 5 miles south and 1 mile east of Alcomdale and 28 miles northwest of Edmonton, on

Wednesday, March 12, 1924

Commencing at 10 A. M. Sharp, the following chattels, to wit:

Horses

1 Team Brown Mares, 7 and 8 yrs. old, weight 2900.
1 Grey Gelding, 6 yrs. old, weight 1450.
1 Black Gelding, 3 yrs. old, weight, 1350.
1 Black Gelding, 2 yrs. old, weight 1200.
1 Sorrel Gelding, 2 yrs. old, weight 1250.
1 Bay Gelding, coming 2 yrs. old, weight 1000.
1 Grey Gelding, 11 yrs. old, weight 1600
1 Black Gelding, 11 yrs. old, weight 1600.
1 Suckling Colt.

Cattle

2 Milk Cows, now milking.
6 Steers, 2 years old.
1 Steer, 3 years old.
6 Heifers, 2 years old.
4 Cows.
5 Calves.

Hogs

2 Yorkshire Brood Sows, 2 years old.

100 Plymouth Rock Chickens.

Household Goods

1 heavy oak Parlor Table.
1 Combination Desk and Book Case.
3 Rocking Chairs. 1 Oak Chiffonier
1 Oak Bed, complete. 1 Oak Dresser.
2 Iron Beds, complete. 1 Cot.
6 Kitchen Chairs. 1 Large Heating Stove.
1 Fire Extinguisher. Several Wall Pictures.
1 Enterprise Lard Press.
1 Enterprise No. 22 Sausage Grinder.
1 Couch, Dishes, Cooking Utensils. Carpet Sweeper.
5 Doz Sealers. Stone Jars, 1 to 20 gallon.
6 qt. Ice Cream Freezer. Cutter. Stretcher.
Clothes Wringer. 2 Congoleum Rugs, 6x9 and 9x12
Oil Stove Heater. 3 Burner Oil Stove, and other small articles too numerous to mention.

Harness

4 Sets Work Harness.
2 Single Harnesses.

Machinery

1 10-20 Case Tractor, in A1 shape.
1 3 Bottom Granitor 14-inch Gang.
1 22-inch Brush Breaker.
1 John Deere 16-inch Sulky.
1 Kentucky 22 Disc Drill.
1 Deering 7 foot Binder
1 Deering 5 foot Mower
2 Deering 10 foot Rakes.
1 Robinson Manure Spreader.
1 John Deere 16-16 Disc
1 Steel Harrow and Cart.
3 Good High Wheel Farm Wagons.
1 Steel Farm Truck.
1 Top Buggy.
1 Democrat Wagon.
3 Extra Buggy Poles.
3 Sets Bob Sleighs.
1 Corn Cultivator.
1 Jumper.
1 Potato Cultivator
1 Acme Hay Sweep.
1 Pump Jack.
1 1½ H.P. Gas Engine and Power Washing Machine.
1 8 H.P. Galloway Engine.
1 8-inch Grinder.
1 26-inch Saw
1 Fanning Mill.
1 DeLaval No. 12 Cream Separator.
1 Complete Gasoline Lighting System.
1 Lawn Mower.
1 Grain Pickler.
1 25 20 Winchester Rifle.
2 12-Gauge Shotguns.
1 Hog Oiler
1 Box Heater.
Several Hay Racks.
Tools, Chains and other things.

Light Four Overland Car, in good shape

Terms Cash, unless otherwise arranged.   Free Lunch at Noon

For information regarding sales call Ball's Stock Yards, 1½ Blocks north of P. O., Phone 1665, Edmonton

J. D. Stevens
Owner

D. A. McMILLAN
Clerk

Chas. E. Walks
Auctioneer

159

CHAPTER SEVENTY-TWO

In the early summer of 1924 my grandparents, dad and Aunt Ellen set out on their long journey by car to Minnesota. According to Aunt Ellen dad did all the driving. The many items they took with them included their trustworthy tent safely secured to the Overland's running board.

I did a mileage calculation and their road trip down involved driving approximately fifteen hundred miles on I assume a lot of dusty gravel roads. Aunt Ellen recalled that on their way down they stopped at Melville, Saskatchewan to visit with the Kirwan family. Uncle Bert at the time was employed with C N R as a dispatcher in Melville. Aunt Ellen particularly remembered the blowing dust and sand they encountered as they crossed portions of Saskatchewan. I don't imagine the side curtains on their Overland car would have been exactly dust proof.

Considering the distance and the primitive condition of the roads in 1924 it was an admirable undertaking. It was made doubly difficult by the fact that it was not easy for grandfather to travel with his serious leg problems. They did not stay in any five star motels but relied on their trustworthy tent for sleeping accommodations. Again I wonder how they managed considering there were not that many developed campsites in those early years.

It had been ten short years since my grandparents had made the journey to their new home in Alberta filled with optimism for the future. They were now going back hoping for a miracle cure for grandfather's serious leg problems. Sadly the Mayo Clinic doctors could not give him an exact diagnosis of what was causing the worsening paralysis in his legs. Having exhausted their medical options my grandparents no doubt started their long journey home with heavy hearts.

There was however one bright spot on their long road trip to Minnesota and South Dakota. They did take time to stop and visit with grandma's sisters and grandfather's brother Henry on their way home. Some of the photo's they took in South Dakota are shown below.

In the first photo below the three youthful looking first cousins appear to be enjoying their time together at the Collins farm. Aunt Ellen and Frank Collins would faithfully keep in touch with each other for the next eighty plus years.

Aunt Ellen, Dad, Frank Collins

In the next photo grandma and her sister Cecilia Miler are shown with Cecilia's two daughters. In the background we get a partial view of the Stevens Overland car's left running board well stocked with their traveling supplies.

Second from Left; Grandma, Sister Ceal, and her two daughters

In the last photo taken at the Collins farm grandma appears to be lost in thought. She is perhaps contemplating the difficult challenges that lie ahead in coping with grandfather's ever worsening medical condition.

Harry Collins Grandfather Grandmother and her sister Alice Collins

CHAPTER SEVENTY-THREE

After their return home from their long excursion the family was faced with caring for grandfather as he condition worsened. They also had the task of resuming farming operations after their 1924 farm sale. Dad never did discuss how they accomplished this apart from the fact they had borrowed some work horses from Mr. Perrott. Fortunately grandma was endowed with a very strong take-charge personality and was able to successfully cope with the challenges the family now faced.

The photo following has grandfather sitting in his recliner chair just outside their south sun porch. As he had lost the use of his legs by then dad no doubt had helped him out to enjoy some sunshine. This is the last photo's we have of grandfather prior to his passing.

There is an interesting history behind how grandfather got his recliner chair. When Aunt Mae and Aunt Margaret began their respective working careers they each saved a portion of their first paycheck. They then invested their combined savings into buying their dad a top of the line recliner chair. They rightly thought that he required a comfortable place to relax after a hard day's work on the farm. Grandfather's chair then made the trip to Alberta with the rest of the family household furniture.

Years later after grandma had passed on it was put in storage. When dad and mom built their Log cabin at the Lake it was moved there and became part of the cabin's furnishings. In 1998 when we tore the cabin down Kevin and Cathy took the chair and had it beautifully restored. Grandfather's old recliner chair now has a place of honor with their other living room furniture.

Dad remembered an incident when they were shipping some pigs to market later that summer. Grandfather was quite concerned about the hogs having sufficient weight to be sent to market. He told me how he had carried grandfather out to inspect the hogs in the stock trailer before the final decision was made to sell them. Dad would have been twenty years old at the time.

CHAPTER SEVENTY-FOUR

After a valiant battle against an unknown disease, grandfather passed away at home on August 10th, 1925 at fifty-eight years of age. His long illness and constant care had been a cross to bear for all the family members and particularly grandma. Interestingly both his parents also passed on in the early part of August, his mother on August 3rd and his father on August 8th.

The following clip I assume was in a Canistota paper that grandma had saved reporting grandfather's passing. John Stevens died at Edmonton, Canada, Monday and is to be buried today. Mr. Stevens was one of the early settlers of this County and lived at the head of "Stevens Hill" until moving to Canada twelve years ago. He has a great many friends among the old settlers here who will regret to hear of his death. His funeral services were held at St. Emmerence Church at Qui Barre with burial in St. Joachim's Catholic Cemetery in Edmonton.

Although we have documented most of grandfather's struggles and triumphs in his life. I would like to review the life of a grandfather I never had the privilege of knowing. Grandfather's journey in life took him a long way from its beginnings at La Crosse, Wisconsin to a farm thousands of miles away in Alberta. In the interval he would experience both happiness and heartbreak which no doubt gave him a strong resolve to face whatever challenges life sent his way.

At twelve years of age grandfather became man of the house when his father passed away on their Minnesota farm. Four years later at sixteen he became head of a family of three younger siblings with the passing of his mother. When we read the few lines he wrote regarding his mother's passing we can feel the pain of the loss when he states. "Mother was 47 years 3 months and 3days old." At the time little did he realize that one of his grandson's would go back one hundred and nineteen years later to locate her exact final resting place thanks to his careful hand written note.

Perhaps one his biggest challenge in his early life was convincing his future father in law that he was worthy of taking his daughter's hand in marriage. However, thankfully, he rose to the challenge and married grandma in spite of great grandfather's objections.

My grandparents' personalities complemented each other very well. Grandma seemed to have inherited many of her father's German genes. Grandfather from all reports exhibited many of his mother's Irish mannerisms. Dad said he never heard grandfather use a swear word which I think speaks volumes about his composure and upstanding character

In his 1918 letters to grandma grandfather showed a genuine concern for her welfare and that of Aunt Irene and her family. Aunt Mae's story describing her happy childhood days on the farm in South Dakota speaks volumes about grandfather's positive attitude and his enjoyment in doing the little things in life. Her words describing her father I think warrant repeating. "The gladness in doing tasks at hand fixed in my childhood by my father never changed throughout my long life. It has given me a feeling of security that untold wealth could not equal"

My grandparents' land mark mid-life decision to move to Alberta and began a new farming venture was admirable. Once in Alberta grandfather became actively involved on the local school board and other community organizations.

As a teenager when visiting with Mr. Cloutier an old timer from the Mearns district recalled how he thought grandfather resembled a minister when he was out in public. I took the comment to mean that grandfather always was well dressed when out and about. This was also indirectly a compliment to grandma who no doubt kept his suits and shirts well pressed long before the era of the local dry cleaners.

Grandfather must have inherited some of his father's musical genes. These were passed down to both Aunt Ellen and Aunt Margaret in their talent for playing the piano. Cousin Gertrude Bohan recalled her mother telling her how grandfather and she would sometimes provide music for local dances, with Aunt Margaret playing the piano accompanied by grandfather on his violin.

Grandfather faced his final struggle in life with resolve and dignity. The paralysis that started in legs would eventually confine grandfather to bed for many months eventually taking his life.

Looking back I am sure the family had a helpless feeling watching grandfather gradually slipping away with a then unknown medical condition. However they could be proud of the many milestones that grandfather together with grandma had achieved during their life together.

John D. Stevens (2nd)

An undated photo of grandfather in his Sunday best south of their home on the farm

CHAPTER SEVENTY-FIVE

After grandfather's death the family continued farming much as I presume grandfather would have wished them to. In 1925 dad was elected to the position of secretary of the Morinville U. G. G. local board the position grandfather had previously held. Dad would go on to be secretary of the Morinville local for forty-nine years until his passing in 1974.

An unexpected opportunity to purchase an additional quarter of land also came up in 1925. How this land acquisition was eventually put together is an interesting story.

The estate of John McGillis owned the one hundred and sixty acres immediately south of my grandparents' home quarter. According to his niece Jean McDonald John had enlisted in the Canadian Army in September of 1916. He was subsequently posted to France where he was killed during the last stages of the World War in June of 1917.

John had purchased the land from the C. P R. that was given thousands of acres as part of the deal for building a railroad across Canada. They then sold it to new settlers who were anxious to begin farming. His estate was now actively seeking a buyer for the land. The executors of John's estate had written grandma inquiring if they were interested in the adjoining land.

In an old letter that I have addressed to grandma the executors of John's estate indicated that a neighbor had made a commitment to buy the land. However they had waited a long period of time and apparently they were no longer interested. They were now offering the land to Dad and grandma for thirty five hundred dollars.

They accepted their offer with Dad borrowing the money from a Mr. Ricard from Morinville for the land purchase. It took a lot of courage to buy more land while they still struggling financially from their 1924 farm sale. The banks in those days frowned on loaning money to anyone but individuals who really did not need it. It took dad many years to pay off this farm land purchase loan.

In 1928 grandma sold one of their original quarter sections grandfather had purchased four miles north of Qui Barre. The buyer was Justin Douziech with a sale price of thirty three hundred dollars. The Douziech family built an impressive two story brick home and raised a family of ten children there. They sold their farm in 1948; however their old two story brick home still remains a very visible landmark on highway #44.

CHAPTER SEVENTY-SIX

Baseball was a big part of rural summer life in Alberta's formative years. Sunday church picnics featured games between neighboring communities with large numbers of devoted fans following their respective teams.

This undated photo following of the Qui Barre baseball team of the 1920's I would assume was taken at the annual St. Emmerence church June picnic. Many of the players pictured in the photo including dad would play ball with the team for many years into the future. Dad is shown wearing his trademark wool sweater which he always had on in future team photos.

Riviere Qui Barre Baseball Team 20's.
Back row left to right: Omer Boddez, John Stevens, Armand Gervais, Fred Caron, Ed Borle.
Front row: Bill Desnoyers, Maurice Boddez, Tom Walsh, Jerry Boddez, Tommy Burgess.

The following two photos were taken while dad was playing baseball at Westlock Sports Day during the summer of 1929. The photo on the left shows Uncle Leonard McNamara, mom and dad. The photo on the right has dad seated on the bumper of their Whippet car. The car was built by Overland car Company and was first brought out in 1926.

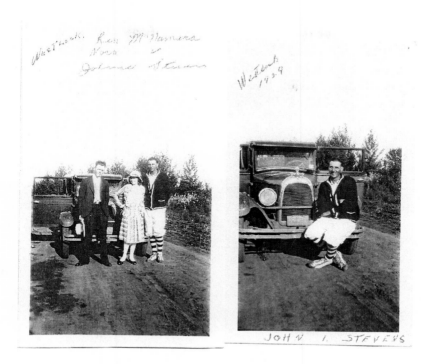

JOHN I. STEVENS

CHAPTER SEVENTY-SEVEN

On November 5th 1929 Aunt Ellen married Angus McGillis at St. Emmerence Church in Qui Barre. Aunt Ellen said it was a small wedding with approximately forty guests attending a wedding breakfast at the Stevens home after their marriage.

A life changing event had occurred just prior their marriage with the stock market collapse of October 1929. The paragraph below confirms what Aunt Ellen often mentioned regarding the hard times they endured beginning shortly after their marriage.

On October of 1929 the stock market crashed wiping millions of dollars of stock equity with the accompanying bankruptcy of many companies. Thousands of people were unemployed and commodity prices crashed including the price farmers received for their products. Wheat that had been a dollar a bushel went down to 33cents with a further drop to 19 cents a bushel by 1932. This period was often referred to as the dirty thirties because of the widespread drought and winds in much of Southern Alberta and Southern Saskatchewan. Economic conditions did not really improve until the beginning of World War two in 1939.

CHAPTER SEVENTY-EIGHT

Grandma saved the following newspaper clipping below sent to her by Aunt Irene updating the fortunes of the Fritz family in 1929. It describes a vacation the Fritz family took to visit family members at Parker, South Dakota.

"Last week Frank Fritz of Raton, New Mexico, visited at the Harry Collins and S. S. Clark homes. He being related to Mrs. Collins by marriage to her niece, who was Miss Irene Stevens, eldest daughter of the late J. D. Stevens.

Mrs. Fritz health began failing twelve years ago and their doctor advised the climate of New Mexico. They made a sale of their farm property and went in search of better health for his wife. The climate proved ideal in her case, along with what is known in that country as the Abrams Electrical Treatment. Mrs. Fritz is now restored to perfect health.

Frank got work with the Atchison Topeka and Santa Fe railroad as an apprentice in boiler making at 24cents an hour. He is still working for the same company and now draws 75 cents per hour as a master mechanic at boiler making. We were glad to shake again with Frank, and to find again the same smiling face. Come again Frank".

I would like to acknowledge the assistance of Cousin Ann Littleton for her help in providing the location of Aunt Irene's beauty Salon in Raton.

We don't know the exact year that she established her hair salon in Raton however by 1930 she had a well established business in the lower level of the Seaberg Hotel in Raton. This further information was provided courtesy of the Raton, Museum. Her shop was listed in big bold black letters in the 1930 Raton phone directory as Fritz's Beauty Shoppe Seaberg B.

The Seaberg Hotel was a large impressive brick building built in 1904 and was first called the Seaberg European Hotel. Following is an undated photo of Raton with the Hotel on the right with Goat Hill looming large in the background.

CHAPTER SEVENTY-NINE

As we mentioned previously the challenge of acquiring the necessary resources to begin farming again after their 1924 sale was not easy. However by the early 1930's they had managed to cobble together the necessary used machinery to operate the farm successfully.

The photo above has dad cutting an excellent looking crop of oats with three horses and a binder. On a good day dad could manage to cut fifteen acres using his binder and three horses.

The photo below has dad's threshing crew filling up the barn loft with straw the easy way. In essence the threshing machine was doing the work blowing the straw into the barn loft. The alternative would have been manually forking it through a side door in the barn loft. Their Whippet car and trailer was also involved in the threshing operation. It is shown with a barrel of fuel on it just to the front of the Case tractor.

The photo following has dad trying out Arlow Rooke's Motor Cycle. He was part of dad's threshing crew that year and liked to test his Motor Cycle's endurance capacity. According to dad he could make the bundles fly in all directions when he hit a stook with his motorcycle at a high speed.

Dad did some custom threshing and one of his more memorable experiences was when he was eating raisin pie after supper one night. Apparently the lighting was not the greatest when he noticed a peculiar looking raisin that on closer examination was a fly. He never said what he did with the fly however I am sure it was well cooked.

CHAPTER EIGHTY

The wheels of time eventually caught up with their old Case tractor. It became time to look for a more modern source of power on the Stevens farm. The unique part of this decision was that their Case tractor remained on the farm. To my knowledge it was one of the few items of machinery that stayed on the farm when a similar piece of new equipment was purchased.

Grandfather and dad certainly couldn't be accused of leaving derelict pieces of old machinery in the back pasture for later generations to clean up. After many years the only remaining evidence of the Case tractor was its large right back rear wheel. It had put into service north of the workshop as a storage area for scrap metal.

In 1998 when we built our new home at the Sandy Lake it was put into service again. It became a large and very durable fire pit on our beach area. The survivable of this old wheel I think is a fitting tribute to the early tractor history on the Stevens farm. It is shown below as the large round blue object in the center our beach area.

We have no records in what year or from whom dad purchased his John Deere D tractor. I would assume it was from August Krauskopf who had the John Deere dealership in Morinville. As we mentioned earlier dad and Aunt Ellen had boarded with the family while attending high school in Morinville.

The John Deere tractor that dad would own for many years had a very interesting history. The John Deere Company manufactured it for thirty years from 1923 to 1953. In later years rubber tires were added plus other cosmetic changes. One of the secrets to the success of their tractor was its simple engine design using twin horizontal cylinders. It had a distinct exhaust sound a rapid-fire pop pop pop that became their trademark.

The reliability of the John Deere D tractors over the many years built up a lot of good will with farmers. The eventual outcome was that the John Deere Company is a leader in the manufacture and sale of farm machinery in the world. As we will discuss later their many items of machinery for sale were always conveniently displayed in their old Farmers Pocket Ledger notebooks. This rather early affordable exposure no doubt helped them in achieving this enviable sales position. I guess now days we could refer to the above as excellent brand recognition.

The excellent sketch of a John Deere D shown plowing below is what dad's tractor would have resembled when it rolled onto the Stevens farm some time in the1930's.

An interesting story was in the Qui Barre history book written by mom. It related to an accident she had operating their new John Deere D tractor while out doing fieldwork. "We had a John Deere tractor, but it was used mostly for crushing grain, plowing and threshing. I remember my first experience with the tractor. I didn't start making the turn in time and took out a stretch of fence. Years later Johnnie gave me a toy model of that tractor which I treasure." Tractors equipped with power steering were along ways into the future in those years. Mom's little green John D Deere shown following is now on display on my office desk.

CHAPTER EIGHTY-ONE

In early June of 1931 Uncle John Franz developed pneumonia very suddenly and passed away on June 12th at the Misericordia Hospital in Edmonton. In that era it was not uncommon for someone who was in excellent physical condition to be struck down suddenly with pneumonia.

Dad remembered going upstairs to Uncle John's room. He discovered he was having a very difficult time breathing. In desperation he told dad to kick the windows out so he could get more air. No doubt his ability to breathe normally had been already seriously comprised. Uncle John was hospitalized however he passed away a few days later. His services were held in St. Joseph's Cathedral in Edmonton with burial in the St. Joachim's Catholic Cemetery close to my grandfather John Stevens's gravesite.

If we fast-forward fifteen years into the future I was in the same predicament as Uncle John. I also was in the Misericordia hospital very ill with pneumonia for a period of three weeks. However thankfully by that time penicillin was available to treat pneumonia and it literally saved my life.

I guess if there was one common theme in Uncle John's life it was one of hard physical labor that was part and parcel of being a carpenter in the twentieth century. At thirty-nine years of age he embarked on the biggest adventure of his life when he came to Alberta to practice his carpentry skills.

The Farmstead that Uncle John built for the Perrott family was for years one of the largest and most impressive building site in the entire Qui Barre district. The barn he built for Kenneth McGillis in the Ray district in 1925 is still in excellent condition as is the large horse barn he built on the MacLeod farm some time prior to 1931.

Barns are not only buildings of Uncle John's to survive into the twenty first century. In speaking with Dennis Belanger recently he indicated that Uncle John had built his father Elphege's home in 1924. Members of the Belanger family are still using the home.

In addition to his expert carpenter skills Uncle John was an excellent butcher. I assume having learned his meat cutting skills at the Franz family butcher shop in South Dakota. When living with my grandparents he put his butchering skills to good use making sausage for the family with his big sausage grinder and lard press. He also helped smoke ham and bacon for the family. The smoke house was located east of grandma's chicken house. As a small boy I was intrigued with its blackened interior walls. One wonders what Uncle John's secret was which prevented the smoke house from going up in flames during the meat curing process.

Aunt Ellen Uncle recalled that Uncle John always kept his butcher knives razor sharp and ready for use. Woe to any family member who used one of his knives without his permission. According to her if they inadvertently did it never passed unnoticed by Uncle John. We are fortunate to still have Uncle John's black leather pouch containing many of his original knives.

Alvin Dhodet an old timer from the Qui Barre district told me humorous incident regarding Uncle John's perhaps supernatural powers. Apparently during a catechism class at St. Emmerence Church the parish priest Father McIntyre asked the class who made the world? One of the young Kramps boys replied that John Franz did. Obviously in his mind Uncle John had built many of the local structures that made up his world.

Another story dad told me about Uncle John was an incident one winter day that happened upstairs in Joe Paquette's Red and White store in Qui Barre. The store had a large top level that had pool tables that served as a gathering area for the men of the local community. The time period we are discussing was sometime during the years in which prohibition was in force. As we discussed early it was a criminal offense to carry liquor on your person or even to consume it. It had been outlawed completely accept when a doctor prescribed it for medical purposes. Your local druggist in effect became the dispenser of alcoholic spirits in the local community. According to some old timers the local doctor was sometimes quite liberal in prescribing alcohol as a cure for many ailments that afflicted his patients.

To get back to our story Uncle John always wore a large heavy overcoat in the winter. According to dad he often had a rolled up newspaper in one of the pockets of his coat. Apparently the police had stopped at the store for some reason. They noticed Uncle John with his large overcoat and what appeared to be a large round package in one of his pockets. They naturally suspected that he had a bottle of forbidden spirits concealed in his coat. They were about to search his person when he told them in no uncertain terms to keep their dam hands off of him. His reason being they had failed to provide the necessary search warrant. In retrospect Uncle John was innocent correctly knowing that he was within his rights in refusing them to search his person. Apparently that strong sense of independence that grandma Stevens often exhibited was also included in her brother John's genes.

By way of background the name of the publication in Uncle John's coat that long ago winter day was The Family Herald and Weekly Star. It was published in Montreal and interestingly grandma saved one of the round cardboard tubes that the paper came which had a date of 2\6\32. The police had good reason to be suspicious of the round object in Uncle John's pocket on that winter day. We would have to assume Uncle John's subscription was paid up for a year when he passed on in 1931. Grandma put Uncle John's empty cardboard paper tube to good use. She neatly rolled up a copy of their 1924 farm sale bill and inserted it in the paper tube for safekeeping. Another old item to survive of Uncle John's is a duplicate copy of the land title issued in 1919 for his Sandy Lake Homestead.

My older cousins have fond memories of Uncle John always having treats for them when he came to visit at their homes. According to Cousin Ron McGillivray his choice of goodies for his nieces and nephews were sticks of Licorice.

Cousin Ron McGillivray related the following story to me about a long ago visit of Uncle John's to Edmonton's summer fair. Apparently Uncle John had brought market hogs into the city with his car and the stock trailer. The trailer was left at McGillivray's while he went to the summer Fair. Ron said Uncle John enjoyed checking out new products that were often offered for sale at the Fair. Proudly Uncle John returned to the McGillivray's with a supposedly unbreakable set of combs that he had purchased at the Fair. At the time Uncle Mac was in the furniture business in Norwood and there was a barn at the back of their lot. Half of it being used for storage and the remainder was a garage. Uncle John anxious to test his supposedly unbreakable combs went out got a hammer from the garage. Sadly the combs did not live up to their indestructible billing and succumbed to his torture test.

We still have Uncle John's carpenter well worn wood tool chest that he brought with him from South Dakota in 1909. It contains many of his original saws, levels and other items. It is a reminder to me of his well-lived life of hard physical labor. Many of the barns and some of the homes that he built have survived into the twenty first century as a testament to his excellent carpenter skills.

To conclude our examination of Uncle John's life I would like to quote the following sentence by Aunt Ellen McGillis where she aptly describes Uncle

John's motto in life of always keeping the bar high. It was part of a section describing his life written by her in the The Wheels of Time History Book. "John Franz was as meticulous about his butchering business as he was about his carpentry".

75-year-old McGillis Barn. Built by Uncle John Franz in 1926

Grandchildren Joe, Cameron, Josh, and Kayla in front of barn August 19th 2001

Uncle John Franz: Undated

CHAPTER EIGHTY-TWO

As we referred to earlier, in the late winter of 1932 grandma developed a severe case of pneumonia similar to what taken Uncle John's life a year earlier. Their local family doctor Dr. Ferguson from Morinville prescribed what was than the standard treatment for pneumonia. It consisted of Mustard plasters being applied at regular intervals and lots of fresh air. Aunt Ellen came back home to assist in caring for grandma. She recalled that they kept the top part of the bedroom windows open at all times so grandma could get lots of fresh air. Aunt Margaret and Aunt Kathryn also came out and helped during grandma' illness. Fortunately after considerable bed rest grandma did recover from her illness. Why grandma recovered from her bout with pneumonia and her brother John did not is one of the mysteries of life. Perhaps the good Lord in his wisdom knew grandma still had important lessons on living yet to be imparted to her grandchildren.

CHAPTER EIGHTY-THREE

On April 25th of 1932 your great grandparents John I. Stevens and Catherine Eleanor McNamara were married at St. Emmerence Catholic Church at Qui Barre. Mom saved the following announcement from I assume from an Edmonton paper in her scrapbook.
Stevens – McNamara

A very quiet but pretty wedding was solemnized in St. Emmerence church, Riviere Qui Barre, on Monday, April 25, when Catherine Eleanor, youngest daughter of Mr. And Mrs. T. J. McNamara became the bride of John Stevens son of Mrs. J. D. Stevens of Morinville. Fr. McIntyre officiated. The bride entered the church on the arm of her father and looked charming in a Chonga weave suit of midnight blue with hat and accessories to match. Margaret McNamara was her sister's bridesmaid and chose as her ensemble a knitted suit and beret of mocha brown, with a fox fur. Leonard McNamara acted as groomsman. The happy couple left immediately after the ceremony on a short motor trip south. They will, on their return make their home on the groom's farm.

A Monday wedding now that's different, we have come a long way to our present day traditional weekend ceremonies. Mom saved her wedding suit, which we still have. She also saved their Registration of Marriage Certificate that among other things inquired if the bride and groom could write. Unfortunately there are no photos available from their wedding day. We do however have some summer scenes of 1932 from grandma's yard of my parents in separate photos looking quite debonair.

Cecelia McAnally
Johnnie Stewart
Margaret McNamara
1932

C. McANALLY
1932

NORR 3

187

For their first two years of married life my parents lived with grandma Stevens in her home on the farm. This arrangement was not that uncommon in the early years. Grandma Joyce's Uncle Jack and Aunt Sis also lived with her Grandma Ledoux on the farm at Albertville, Saskatchewan after their marriage.

CHAPTER EIGHTY-FOUR

As we discussed earlier during the summer months baseball was a major part of any weekend activity. The photo of the 1932 Mearns baseball team shows dad as a team member with Walter Fitzgerald to his left and on the far right of the front row is Lefty Lutz. Their coach (manager) was Fr. Stacey who was then the parish priest at Mearns shown on the far left of the back row. The cars in the background would indicate the photo was taken at the annual St. Charles church picnic after the team had won the ball tournament.

MEARNS BASEBALL TEAM 1932

I have a gut feeling that the Qui Barre team for some reason was not invited to play at the Mearns picnic that day. Fr. Stacey being an astute coach brought some extra players in for the day with obviously good results. The cash prize for winning the tournament no doubt assisted in the parish's finances.

In this photo dad is again wearing his trademark wool sweater as he was in the first Qui Barre baseball team photo. Perhaps grandma was responsible for knitting these sweaters for dad. When he passed away he still owned a nice light tan front button sweater that he wore for semi dress occasions.

The baseball team photo was among family keepsakes that I loaned to the committee that published the Mearns History Book that they included it in their book.

CHAPTER EIGHTY-FIVE

This 1932 Stevens yard photo below shows the relatively new family's Whippet car. The Whippet was huge step up from their old Overland car. The former Overland car Company built it. John Willys Knight who was originally associated with Overland Car Company had assisted in its design. Their first models were built in 1926.

The gentleman pictured sitting on the fender is Lefty Lutz who was then working for Dad. Lefty was an excellent ball player excelling at pitching. His home was on a farm in the Busby area. On weekends he would walk four half miles north of our farm to the N. A. R. rail line to the Peace River country and use it as a quick way home to Busby.

I have vague memories of riding in the Whippet with Mom. We would often go to visit my maternal grandparents who lived on a farm a half mile south of Qui Barre. Aunt Mary Ann McNamara recalled yours truly standing up in the back seat of the Whippet when we stopped at her dad's Red and White store in Qui Barre. In that era passengers riding in a car were not required to be restrained by anything such thing as a seat belt.

The Whippet did double duty in that it was often used in transporting supplies and livestock. As we referred to earlier many loads of pigs were hauled to market in Edmonton with the Whippet and trailer.

The first photo following shows dad and cousin Fee all decked out in their Sunday best south of grandma's front veranda. The second photo was taken north of the house with dad in his Sunday best smoking one of his trademark roll your own cigarettes. Too bad we did not have color photography then to capture the beauty of grandma's flowers and shrubs.

CHAPTER EIGHTY-SIX

In 1934 Dad and Mom built a small story and half home at the very south
end of the farmyard that they would live in for the next thirty-eight years.

A summer photo shows Mom standing in the front porch of their little
house on the prairie with a hanging flower basket (Home grown) plus other
flowers growing in front and along the south side of the house. The outdoor
biffy is in the far left hand corner of the photo looking quite lonely all by
itself on the flat prairie landscape.

1935
Mora Stevens

Also in 1934 grandma went back to South Dakota to reconnect with her sisters Alice and Cecilia or Ceal as grandma affectionately always referred to her. I have memories of grandma getting letters from the states and they always seemed to be from her sister Cecelia.

As we discussed earlier grandma and her two sisters had been through a lot together. Beginning with their childhood days in Iowa and ending with the family's final move to their new farm. Although grandma never recorded any written comments of her trip I am sure it was very special for her. Sadly it would be the last time the three sisters would have the opportunity to be together.

193

Mrs. J. D. Stevens   Mrs. Harry Collins   Mrs. Casper Miller

CHAPTER EIGHTY-SEVEN

  In the early 1930's when grandma was in her sixties she decided to buy a car. She no doubt correctly assumed that owning a car would give her a lot more independence. Grandma was always a kind of take-charge lady. She no doubt had little difficulty in mastering the art of driving a car.

The only photo we have of grandma's car is a summer photo in 1937. In it she is shown sitting on the running board of her car proudly holding her grandson Kenneth McGillis pictured below.

June 1937

Cousin Ron McGillivray told me grandma enjoyed attending local baseball games. She would park her car behind the backstop and remain there the entire day thoroughly enjoying the ball games.

Unfortunately grandma was involved in an accident when going to church one Sunday morning. Apparently she ran into or over MaryAnn Paquette who thankfully did not suffer any serious injuries. MaryAnn recently celebrated her hundredth birthday that I think would confirm her lack of any ill effects from long ago accident.

195

In grandma's defense MaryAnn was always a very slight individual. She perhaps would not have loomed large on the roadway on that long ago Sunday morning. Grandma was fortunate in that some goodwill already existed between the Stevens and Paquette families. Joe Paquette MaryAnn's father owned the local Red and White store. He had been a good friend of Uncle John Franz and had served as a Pall Bear at his funeral services. Unfortunately I think grandma's Sunday morning accident marked the end of her driving days.

CHAPTER EIGHTY-EIGHT

After my parents built their new home at the far end of our farmyard in 1934 grandma was now living alone in her large farmhouse. As our previous stories about her indicated she was no shrinking violet as far as confronting any emergency that came up. Grandma's take-charge personality is clearly illustrated in the following story regarding implementation of her back up security measure.

Grandma's dog was always housed just outside the back porch door to alert her of any middle of the night intruders. However now that she was living alone she may have thought an extra home security measure might be in order.

Grandma rightly assumed that any extra security measure should be very accessible and ready for use in the evident of an emergency. She concluded that just in case she would install her back up security underneath the pillow in her bed. I recall dad telling me that grandma periodically made sure her backup security was in good working order.

Grandma's portable backup security system was small compact Dellinger handgun. I assume that both the small handgun and grandfather's pistol made the journey up with the other family belongings from South Dakota in 1914.

The time frame that grandma initiated her extra security measure coincided with handgun registration becoming compulsory in Canada. However I have a feeling that grandma never registered her gun with any Canadian Government Agency. Grandma may have assumed that she had the right to bear any kind of firearm in Canada as she previously had done while living in the South Dakota.

Fortunately grandma never had the occasion to use her little back up security device. The outcome I fear might have been grandma one and intruder 0.

Harold Granger recently told one of grandma's long forgotten random acts of kindness to me when I called him regarding another matter.

In 1932 Harold whose mother had recently passed away was living with his sister and brother on a farm mile and half south of the farm. Harold at the time was in grade one at Belle Valley School and passed the farm on his way to and from school every day.

Harold remembered particularly on summer afternoons on his return home from school grandma would often be waiting for him at the gate with cookies and cold drink. Considering this random act of kindness happened seventy-five years ago Harold has never forgot grandma's kindness.

CHAPTER EIGHTY-NINE

The following article was in The Wheels of Time History Book written by Msgr. W. P. Fitzgerald. It describes how the game of baseball evolved in the Qui Barre community. Although we previously briefly mentioned dad's baseball playing days the following story gives us much more in depth picture of how baseball evolved into a major attraction in this small prairie community.

It seems from its very beginning Riviere Qui Barre has been a baseball centre. Just how did this tradition begin? Rusty Roberts tells it this way:

"There strict Sunday laws on the books at the turn of the century. Among other things Sunday baseball was forbidden and since there no Mounties to ride herd, it was the duty of the Justice of the Peace to see that proper respect was shown for the Lord's Day.

Well, we had a ballgame going on a Sunday afternoon when Joe Poirier, the J. P. at the time came over to straighten out the younger generation by reminding them that they were infringing on the sacred traditions of society.

He stuck out his chin and asked if we didn't know it was Sunday and that baseball was forbidden on the Sabbath. Mr. Poirier thought that would settle the matter right there and then, but it didn't. Bill Perrott spoke up: "Mr. Poirier, you know that nine points make a law." Mr. Poirier couldn't argue with this gem of wisdom, so he nodded assent. "Well," says Bill, "there are nine men on each team and we voted to have a ball game."

My grandma McNamara's three brothers Bud, John and Tommy Kinsella were all members of the above described baseball team. Their love of baseball would stay with the three Kinsellas for their remaining years.

Msgr. Fitzgerald continues his story, The Justice of the Peace counted them and sure enough there were nine in each team, so he shook his head and walked away. From that day to this the residents of Qui Barre have enjoyed their Sunday afternoon baseball.

As we discussed earlier the collapse of the world economies in 1929 had severe repercussions on commodity prices that in turn had a dire effect on the farm economy. This affected every facet of a farm family's life with little money available for recreational expenses. However the Qui Barre baseball and softball teams managed to keep going.

Uniforms became a big issue to the Qui Barre baseball team in that the old ones were wearing out and where was the money going to come from to purchase new ones? Dances were held to raise funds plus Joe Paquette the local storekeeper donated some money towards new uniforms. However they were far short of having sufficient funds to buy new cloth uniforms.

However they decided to buy binder canvass that was used on binders for cutting grain.

Binder canvass was a very course hard material and had to be soaked in water for several hours to soften it. Then it was bleached to bring it as close as possible to the white of the red and white worn by the RQB team. The wife of the Qui Barre baseball team manager Mrs. Phil Caron did all this work and sewing.

The following is a quote from part of the article on the resourcefulness of Mrs. Caron and the effort required to come up with new uniforms for the baseball team. "Before long the operation got on the way, a long uniform for John Stevens who was six foot four, a short one for Jerry Boddez, a stout one for Ed Borle and Armand Pelletier and the rest more or less average size to fit the common man.

While the sewing operation was in progress another trip to Edmonton was made. Twelve pairs of red and white socks at 65cents a pair and twelve red caps at 85cents each with an extra 35cents for the letter proudly displayed over the peak for a total investment of five dollars per suit. A tremendous investment at the time but a good one when not only the team but the whole community needed something to build morale. The new uniforms made their first appearance at a tournament at St. Albert on a Sunday afternoon and the team outdid themselves that day to justify the expense of their new outfits."

Mom kept Dad's Qui Barre baseball uniform from those early years. She did this perhaps in recognition of the time and effort required to make them. We still have it downstairs which is a tribute to their pioneer can do attitude.

She pinned the following note on dad's old baseball suit. "This baseball suit was John I. Stevens made by Mrs. Phil Caron in 1932. The R.Q.B. team wore red caps and red and white socks with the suits and looked real sharp. They played good ball and had good times". The above photo of dad wearing his new baseball suit was taken some time in the summer of 1933.

The following article was in the Wheels of Time History Book concerning the precarious financial situation of the early Qui Barre baseball team budget.

The financial problem was always raising its ugly head in the 30's. Nora Stevens came up with a few records kept by her late husband, John Stevens, who played centre field and acted as Treasurer for the club. The item is captioned "Moneys received in the summer of 1930"

Left over from 1929 (W. P. Fitzgerald)	13.00
Collection from (June 22)	4.85
(Tournament winnings)	
St. Albert Picnic (June 29)	10.00
Villeneuve (July 27)	10.00
Alcomdale (July30)	10.00
Busby Picnic (August 31)	15.00
Fort	2.00
Collection (not dated)	5.65
Earle Howe	.25
Total receipts	70.75
Expenses for summer	56.10
Balance	14.65

The ten-dollars items represented top money in tournaments that year. The second place team got $5.00 to split among them or put in their treasury and the third team got 2.00 to help pay for gasoline. Busby somehow came up with a fifteen-dollar prize, probably because the United Farmers of Alberta backed them. (Governing political party in Alberta in 1930's).

Baseball had come a long way by the time the picture following was taken at a tournament at Alberta Beach. Phil Caron's recruits of the 1920's were now veterans. The team was a credit to the canvass uniforms that were growing softer and whiter with age. But these were only secondary concerns; the important thing was that of improving the caliber of play, developing team spirit, and providing finances to keep the team going.

Back row left to right: Ed Borle, John Stevens, Oscar Blais, Byran Howell and Walter Fitzgerald.
Front row: Jerry Boddez, Octave Pelletier, Maurice Boddez and Andre Boddez. Standing at the back wearing his vest, white shirt, tie and hat is manager Phil Caron.

CHAPTER NINETY

The family dog had to have been one of the most accommodating animals on the farm. They required little recognition for the twenty-four hour sentry service they provided for the farm.

The first family dog photo shows a small Collie pup in its dog house in South Dakota. From the admiring looks of some of the younger Stevens family members it is evident the young puppy is not lacking for love or attention. I have a sneaking suspicion that this was the Collie dog that made the trip to Alberta with the Stevens family.

In the photo below Aunt Ellen is showing off some of her dogs with the help of grandfather. Grandma made the following comment on the back of the photo, "Ellen had to have a picture of her dogs taken". As the following stories indicate the Stevens family dogs would continue their important roles in every day farm life.

J.D. Stevens, daughter Ellen & her dogs

I am indebted to cousins Ron McGillivray and Myra Morin for recalling the fate of a big hairless St. Bernard of grandma's called Scotty. Myra indicated that grandma was very attached to Scotty. She would even let him come into the kitchen on occasion for a special treat. He would look up at the far end of the kitchen cupboard where grandma kept her cookies. Grandma would then open the cupboard door and proceed to give Scotty a cookie from her cookie jar. He would then go back outside happy to have received his treat.

Scotty was not without his faults that included chasing grandma's chickens. With each encounter with a chicken he would remove a tail feather. He persisted and eventually grandma had numerous chickens minus all their tail feathers.

On one of his visits to grandma's Ron had brought his B. B. gun along. Grandma suggested that perhaps a pellet in the rear might discourage Scotty from chasing the chickens. Apparently it worked and when Ron was going home grandma requested that Ron leave his gun with her. She indicated that she would use it if the opportunity presented itself.

True to form Scotty began chasing grandma's chickens again. In her haste to stop Scotty grandma grabbed the twenty-two instead of Ron's B. B. gun. As they say the rest is history as far as her dog Scotty was concerned. Grandma felt terrible and in retrospect I can visualize how it happened considering the many guns that were standing upright in the gun rack in her back porch.

The photo following shows cousin Fee in grandma's back yard looking not too pleased with Scotty's attention seeking ways. In the background it appears grandma had her usual bountiful garden.

The general consensus among the family was that grandma should have another dog to replace Scotty. Another shorthaired St. Bernard dog was found for grandma. Cousin Myra Morin said that grandma's new dog in his excitement to greet you often unsuspectingly placed his front paws in your mid section. Myra mentioned that she always took along a stick along to prevent him from jumping up on her on the two mile round trip to pick up grandma's mail.

In this 1940 photo taken just west of our house grandma's big dog appears to be in one of his more subdued moments. I am looking quite happy resting my arm on his back. My little dog Rex had no doubt had disappeared into his doghouse when grandma's big dog appeared on the scene. I have a theory that grandma thought her new dog might do some serious harm when jumping up on unsuspecting individuals. Perhaps her main concern was her four-year-old grandson who was now under foot a lot around the farmyard. Unfortunately I have no recollection of grandma's second big friendly St. Bernard dog. The fact that I have no memory of grandma's dog indicates to me he was confined to his doghouse most of the time. I think grandma eventually found a new home for her exuberant big St. Bernard.

Some time later when I started school grandma went back to the Stevens family favorite dog a black and white Collie. Again some kind person had given him to her fully grown eliminating grandma the exasperating task of training a new dog. I also assume that her dog already had been given the name Pat when arrived on the farm. One of my lasting memories of Pat was how he would wait for me at our north farmyard gate on my return from school every day. He was an excellent dog with the livestock and also provided great companionship for grandma. Although at times I am sure dad was of the opinion that having two dogs for one farm was not really necessary. The photo following shows Pat greeting me as I arrived home from Belle Valley School in grade one.

Grandma had Pat for at least four years however as our dogs got older Rex and grandma became less compatible. Our former hired man Otto Schroder was now farming on his own. Otto being a bachelor was in desperate need of good dog both for livestock and companionship. Grandma in her generosity graciously agreed to let Otto have Pat.

Of all grandma's dogs her last dog was by far my favorite. She was a small yellow and white female dog called Snipe. Similar to her last dog Snipe was already named and full grown when grandma got her. I have no idea what the circumstances were but perhaps grandma was just being a Good Samaritan in giving her a home. Snipe was a very well trained and intelligent dog. She and grandma seemed to form a strong bound between them.

My fondest memory of grandma's last dog was the surprise package that she presented us with. Exactly who ascertained that Snipe had a new family hidden somewhere on the farm I don't recall. Grandma and dad seemed quite content to wait for her to bring her new family out for our inspection. However I was much more impatient and did some detective work as to the possible location of her new family.

On several occasions I noticed Snipe disappearing under our combination granary and cow barn just west of grandma's house. Over the years the east part where the grain was stored had settled considerably. Dad gave me assurances that the area was accessible only to Snipe. When I peered underneath all I could see was total darkness. However I secretly thought perhaps I should at least attempt to explore this dark dungeon looking area.

I faced another challenge in entering this forbidden area so to speak was that there was thirty years of grain dust had accumulated underneath the granary. Grain dust and I were far from being compatible. The thought of having a bad asthma attack however did not deter me from entering this dark dusty area.

So one morning when dad was in the field and grandma and mom were busy doing their Monday morning clothes wash I decided it was time for action. I began my stomach crawl forgetting completely that my dirt black clothes would soon reveal my ulterior motives to everyone. I persisted and was able to squeeze beneath the granaries large supporting wood crossbeams. I finally located Snipe's new family of puppies in the far northwest corner of the area under the granary. I managed to bring out two pups and Snipe decided after

208

a short while to bring the other two out for our inspection. I don't recall any dire consequences of getting my clothes extremely dusty and dirty. I was totally thrilled at having the puppies now accessible to admire and play with. In my bliss I was totally unaware of much bigger challenge I would soon have to face. The photo following shows me sitting on the east side of the granary with two of Snipes new family. Both the pups and their new handler appear to be enjoying each other's company.

According to dad the farm could not sustain the additional dogs. I reluctantly agreed that we would have to find homes for the new dogs. Cousin Anne Otterson agreed to take one of my favorites that I had named Rex.

In our search for ideas of how to find homes for the remaining puppies dad suggested we bring them to church on Sunday. Often on Sunday's after services the parishioners spent time visiting with neighbors. Dad may have arranged the after Mass Sunday morning puppy swap; however if he had I was totally unaware of it. How it unfolded is described in the paragraph below.

Sunday rolled around with the three remaining pups accompanying us to church. After services Mr. Mullen McRae selected my remaining favorite pup for which he gave me a whole fifty cents. Albert Roy's store was immediately across the street from the church and was always open after Mass on Sunday. After thanking Mr. McRae for his unexpected kindness I promptly ran across the road to spend some of my newfound wealth. I can't recall who the good Samaritans were who took the other puppies home.

Mr. McRae, our parish priest and dad were at the time were the only individuals who openly admitted to voting conservative in the federal elections. So politics in around about way may have entered into our after Church puppy exchange.

Sadly have we no photos of grandma with any her favorite dogs. Grandma I think was of the opinion that having her photograph taken with the family dog was not a very high priority item. So in conclusion of our discussion on the many Stevens family dogs I thought it might be appropriate to have an early 1940 photo of grandma's red and white doghouse. As an added bonus a group of grandma's younger grandchildren are featured sitting on the dog house roof in this late summer snap shot. By their facial expressions the time spent at grandmas during their summer holidays was a happy one.

Ann Otterson, Jack Kirwin, Rita May McGillivray, Bryan Kirwin, Ken McGillis

CHAPTER NINETY-ONE

I want to thank all my cousins again who so willingly agreed to share their special memories of grandma. Particularly when they stayed with grandma during their summer holidays on the farm. Some of these recollections have been mentioned in previous chapters. However there are more stories that I think should definitely be included in our family history.

In a recent conversation with Gertrude Bohan she recalled her and Myra Morin agreeing to disagree while playing up in grandma's attic during their summer holidays.   Before recounting the actual story I will attempt to describe the setting of that long ago afternoon when the two cousins were playing together in grandma's attic.

Grandma's farmhouse was what you could describe as a story and half home. The upstairs was accessed from a door located in the northeast corner of her dinning room. If I recall correctly the stairs were quite steep going up to the second level. I assume the small black pieces of rubber that grandma had attached to the center area of each step were there for wear and safety purposes. At the top landing the attic door was immediately on the right. To gain access to the Attic there was quite a step down to the attic's floor level as cousin Rita Mae O'Brien recently reminded me of. The attic was a long rectangular area with sidewalls sloping about forty-five degrees in configuration with the house rooflines above. Directly below the attic were grandma's dining room and the kitchen.

As a small boy when I entered grandma's attic the many strange looking objects stored there had an aura of mystery to me. The strange looking old odd shaped trunks and the families well traveled tent were really the only objects I could identify.

Getting back to our original topic of Gertrude recollections of their afternoon spent in grandma's attic apparently an impasse developed between the two cousins. To resolve their differences amicably a decision was made to draw a chalk line down the center of the attic floor. To quote a popular expression they perhaps each needed their own space. After having defined their own respective space in the attic Gertrude decided to go down stairs and see how grandma's cooking making was progressing. According to Gertrude Myra wrongly assumed that Gertrude had locked the latch on the outside of the Attic door when she left. After a considerable period of time had gone by grandma called up "for gosh sakes Myra come down stairs". Much to Myra's surprise she discovered the attic door was unlocked. Hopefully Myra then realized that her cousin Gertrude was not such a bad person after all.

According to Gertrude she sensed that grandma sometimes gave preferential treatment to some of her grandchildren. This seemed to occur when it came time to send cookies back home after the grandchildren's visits to the farm. The two chosen ones whose cookie bags appeared to be sometimes a little more bulky to Gertrude were her brother Fee and cousin Ronald. The boy's response regarding grandma's favoritism was that the girls were spared from cleaning out grandma's chicken house. Cousin Myra Morin has also a special memory of grandma still wanting to send cookies home even in her later years.

As the years rolled around Aunt Kathryn and Aunt Margaret thought it was too much work for grandma to be baking batches of cookies to send back with the now older grandchildren to the city. Myra recalled on instance where the family was all in the car and ready to leave for home. Apparently grandma stuck her head in the car window and inquired what was she going to do with all the cookies she had baked.

I assume her cookies were quickly packaged up and sent on their way with the family. I don't think grandma ever completely did give up making cookies.

Gertrude also recalled another incident at grandma's that yours truly was involved in. In an effort to cool off on a hot summer afternoon some of the grandchildren began spraying each other with their water guns. Whether accidentally or deliberately grandma was the victim of a random stream of water from some one's water gun. Grandma quickly established that I was the guilty party. According to Gertrude grandma's method of punishment was swift and very direct. She proceeded to get a pail of water from her nearby rain barrel and promptly deposited on yours truly head. Grandma's motto in life needless to say was actions always speak louder than words that she never hesitated to put it into practice.

Perhaps my best memory of summer days spent at Grandma's was our activities centered around her hammock. Grandma had her hammock suspended between two spruce trees immediately north of the house. With the icehouse immediately to the west it was always a cool shaded area on a hot summer day. I always had the perception that grandma's hammock was a long ways from the ground. However this idea no doubt was formed from the many occasions the hammock occupants ended up on the ground below.

In talking with Cousin Anne Otterson recently she recalled some special memories of times spent with grandma during her summer holidays.

Anne said grandma was very organized in her approach to doing the daily chores. We would all have to agree that grandma excelled at being very good taskmaster. Their mornings were taken up with whatever required doing. I assume this would have included weeding the garden, feeding the chickens and general housework. The last task would have had to be done without the aid any of our modern day kitchen conveniences such as fridges or running water. However, once their morning chores were finished, according to Anne, their afternoons had a much more leisurely pace to them. In fact in Anne's mind it seemed as if they kind of took the afternoon off.

One of the activities that grandma and Anne did in the evenings to relax was reading. On a dull or rainy evening attempting to read by grandma's wall lamps presented a problem. Anne remembers dad volunteering to get the high-test gas lamp working for them. This required a certain level of expertise that began by pumping air into the bottom chamber of the lamp. Then carefully lighting the lamp and adjusting the gas valve that controlled the mantle so it emitted the maximum amount of light. This task was one of the joys of farm living prior to the arrival of electricity.

One certain night as a bed time snack Anne remembers grandma and her enjoying a brick of Neapolitan ice cream. For the younger generation if I recall correctly the brick was packaged in a cardboard container slightly larger than a pound of butter. For the uninitiated Neapolitan ice cream had three layers of ice cream, chocolate, strawberry and vanilla. Eating a brick of "store bought" ice cream as grandma referred to it was a real novelty to her and a treat she really enjoyed. For most of grandma's life the only ice cream readily available had been made by turning the handle on their ice cream maker. However things on the farm changed with the sale of the dairy cows in 1939.This resulted in farm cream no longer being available year around to make ice cream. Living in the country far from a store presented a problem when purchasing a perishable product such as ice cream.

However an obliging gentleman named Ovide Gosslein who ran a Confectionary Store in Morinville solved their distance dilemma. He developed a procedure that assured ice cream would still resemble its original form when it arrived back at the farm. If I close my eyes I can still see Ovide meticulously wrapping each brick with many layers of old newspaper. Taking a piece of white string that hung from a large ball from the ceiling he would then carefully secure the string around the outer layer of newspaper. His careful packaging technique for ice cream bricks endeared him to his many rural customers. Grandma would continue to enjoy her fresh "bought" bricks of ice cream particularly during the hot summer months for her remaining years on the farm.

Cousin Ron McGillivray related the following experience he had at neighboring farm in what now days could be described as the work of a pest control officer.

Apparently our immediate farm neighbors to the south the Falls family had a problem with pigeons making their home in the loft of their barn. Pigeons were a perennial problem in many farm barn lofts with various methods of removal being attempted over the years. Whether Ron volunteered or the Falls family asked for his assistance, I am not sure. However I have a sneaking suspicion that grandma volunteered his services. Grandma was never shy about discussing the abilities and accomplishments of her grandchildren whenever the opportunity presented itself.

Armed with grandma's recommendation and his trust worthy B. B. gun Ron went into action. According to Ron his pigeon hunting was very successful. As an added bonus he received five cents for every bird he reduced their pigeon flock by. Interestingly the Falls barn where Ron had his long ago pigeon hunt was built by Uncle John Franz in 1922. To Uncle John's credit some eighty-seven years later the horse barn is still standing.

As Myra mentioned in our stories about grandma's dogs going to get the mail at the south corner often was a daily task of the grandchildren when visiting grandma during the summer months. Cousin Ron McGillivray remembers one occasion when a very large heavy box full of ladies dresses arrived in the mail for grandma. Apparently the contents were from Aunt

215

Irene Fritz who because of the nature of her work in her beauty salon had ladies clothes to spare. According to Ron the contents were very much appreciated by family members. As we mentioned previously grandfather had selected a farm on high ground a mile north of the main east west road. Many old timers often suggest that when walking to school in their youth it was uphill both ways. However it was definitely uphill most of the way from the mail box up to the farm. Ron was fortunate that day because his cousin Fee had accompanied him to get the mail. Ron particularly remembers how they both struggled in carrying the large heavy box of clothing uphill to grandma's house on the farm.

Cousin Fee Otterson spent considerable time at grandma's during the summer months in his early teenage years. Fee often mentions a memorable afternoon when he stopped by to visit at my parents little home at the far south end of the farmyard. That particular afternoon mom had just finished baking her weekly batch of bread. Mom always made a pan of delicious cinnamon rolls after she finished baking bread. The alluring aroma of her fresh cinnamon buns would no doubt have been present in her small kitchen when Fee arrived.

Mom's kitchen had a very large McCleary cook stove with the white enamel trim. It had a very commanding presence in her small kitchen. She always placed her freshly baked cinnamon buns on a large white platter. The platter was strategically located on a cabinet counter right next to the kitchen table. Assuming Fee was seated at the table I am sure the fresh platter of cinnamon rolls appeared quite tantalizing to him.

Mom being a gracious host no doubt suggested Fee help himself to a nearby cinnamon roll. The sample must have of tasted good so Mom suggested Fee have another one. According to Fee's recollections he willing kept accepting mom's invitation to have another cinnamon bun. Whether all the white was showing on the bottom of the platter with the cinnamon rolls or not we don't know. Apparently Fee did not suffer any ill effects from his marathon cinnamon roll sampling session. In later years Fee sometimes has a slight sense of remorse for his long ago uncontrolled appetite. Mom being an understanding soul no doubt understood most teenage boys have ravenous appetites particularly when it came to eating oven fresh cinnamon rolls. As an added note Fee we still have Mom's white platter on display downstairs from which she served you the many samples of her delicious cinnamon rolls on that long ago summer afternoon.

Another late summer activity that both Fee and Ron recall doing while at grandma's during their summer holidays was picking Saskatoon berries with mom. In that era there was no such thing as planted tame Saskatoon bushes. The Saskatoon bushes were often located along the fence lines that separated neighboring farms. If the neighbors didn't mind you often had to crawl through the barbwire fences to gain access the other side of the tall Saskatoon bushes. Both Ron and Fee remember what a good sport mom was when she accompanied them on their berry picking expeditions. Mom would continue to pick berries every summer until well into her seventies.

In a recent conversation with Cousin Ron McGillivray he said that during his life he had the opportunity to travel extensively. However he indicated that perhaps his fondest memories of vacations where the times spent in his younger years during the summer months at the Stevens farm.

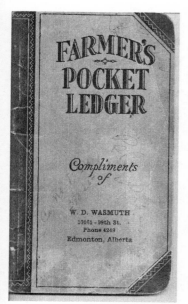

CHAPTER NINETY-TWO

In the following chapter I will attempt to describe what we now consider family keepsakes. They somehow at the conclusion of their useful working days avoided the recycle bin. I have to admit I may have been guilty for not disposing of some of the following items. Grandma used the farmer's pocket ledger shown above in the 1932 to track the farm's financial progress. This little book was the preferred choice of many farmers in the 1930's for keeping tabs on their meager farm finances. The Pocket Ledger's biggest attraction to the cash starved farmers was its affordability. The local John Deere Dealer handed them out to all comers. The second reason for its popularity was the wealth of information it contained which was invaluable in the running of the farm. Included on the back cover was a handy calendar with all the months of the current year listed. Lastly it had many illustrations of farm equipment available for sale from the John Deere Company. This added information however subtle was no doubt a successful form of advertising for the John Deere Company.

Interestingly we still have a one-horse cultivator that was illustrated in grandma's old Ledger book. For some reason it has managed to survive long after its working days were over. It is now on display at Kevin and Cathy's yard in Cardiff.

Why this old book survived perhaps could be summed up by the old adage waste not want not. In other words there were still unused pages available for use on another day. Not in grandma's wildest imagination would she have visualized anyone three quarters of century later attempting to dissect her old book keeping entries. The small print on the front page indicated the book was supplied by John Dealer W. D. Wasmuth 10161-99th St. Phone 4249 Edmonton, Alberta. The address reflected a convenient town down Edmonton location with easy access for farmers when they were in the city.

The expense items in grandma's book far exceeded the income entries. To me this indicated farming has not changed much in the eighty plus intervening years. Grandma was very diligent in her recording all their personal and farm expenses items. The majority of their business was done locally at Morinville, Qui Barre and Mearns.

 Her records also indicate there was an occasional city trip for farm supplies. While in town they no doubt stopped to see the Otterson and McGillivray families. One of the stores they bought farm supplies at while in the city was Eaton's. The second outlet was that venerable old hardware on ninety seventh street the WW Arcade now home to The Hardware Grill. On a personal note the one thing, which I can recall most vividly about the old W. W. Arcade Hardware, was their oily black well-worn wooden floors.

It would be years into the future before the dollars stores would make their appearance. However judging by grandma's records they would have prospered in 1934. Among the endless list of items you could buy for less than dollar were a meal at forty cents, a broom fifty cents, kettle ninety cents, razor blades twenty five cents, flashlight one dollar, Chicago Herald ten cents, loaf of bread twelve cents, a jug of vinegar fifty five cents, a can of Tuckkett's tobacco seventy five cents and a gallon of gas forty five cents. (Pump price in city).

Binder Twine was one of the larger farm expenses that sold for six dollars and forty-five cents per hundred pounds. Tractor fuel (Distillate) was also a large expense at twelve dollars a barrel or twenty-six cents a gallon.

The fuel was bought from Emile Norbert who had a store and bulk gas business in Mearns. It was a small hamlet located about four and half miles north east of the farm. It was established when the railroad went through the area in 1914 to the Peace River Country.

Farmers complain about machinery parts prices today however they were also very high in 1934. Grandma had one entry for binder repairs at Jack Graff's machinery agency in Morinville for twelve dollars, a big expense in 1930 dollars. Jack had a large International Harvester dealership in Morinville. In the early years Jack toured the district with a horse and buggy accompanied by a driver promoting and selling his machinery. In later years he graduated to using a car for getting around the local area. How he ended up in a predominately French speaking town far from his South Dakota roots I don't know. Apparently Uncle John Franz and Jack got along well because Jack was one of the casket bearers at Uncle John's funeral services.
On the income side of the Ledger grandma had many entries for grain sales. There net return after paying trucking charges was around twenty-five cents a bushel for barley and twenty cents for oats.

One bright spot in their grain farming operations now was that UGG had a new grain elevator at Mearns. Before that all UGG customers had to haul their grain to Morinville a considerable longer distance. As we referred to earlier in1928 the UGG elevator in Morinville had been dismantled and rebuilt in Mearns. Grandfather and the rest of the UGG local board had lobbied for years to have an elevator located there. Sadly grandfather was no longer around to see his efforts rewarded with an outlet much closer to home.

Another area there were numerous entries was hog sales. The average price received was approximately ten dollars a hog. As we mentioned previously they were hauled to market in their trailer behind the Whippet. Mom relayed a story to me how on one of their trips to the city they had a mishap and several hogs escaped. Dad managed to herd them to a local farmer's yard where they were reloaded making the rest of the trip to the city safely. There were no entries for eggs sales perhaps because any eggs for sale were traded for groceries.

Grandma had an entry of a dollar a month to Lucerne Dairy for a permit fee. I assume the permit was required to ship butter and cream. As there were no entries for butter or cream sales I would assume that Lucerne sent them a monthly or yearly summary of their sales. If I remember correctly dad mentioned there was a yearly inspection of their dairy barn was required. The Holstein dairy cows were sold in 1939 however the white wash on the dairy barn walls gleamed for many years afterward. Sadly grandma did not consider weather or crop conditions of the current crop year important enough to record. She entered what items she thought were deemed important to the successful running of the farm. Grandma 's motto was perhaps just the facts Mame, just the facts as Joe Friday used to say on the T.V. Program Dragnet.

The only item we have left from the farm's cow milking days that has not been discarded is the 1927 De Laval # 12 Cream Separator. The operating manual also survived with the notation on the front cover in big bold letters "Hang Near Separator" a good piece of advice. The back cover had a large photo of their   factory at Peterborough, Ontario called General Canadian Works of The De Laval Company. The inside of the back cover had hundreds of names of satisfied De Laval customers in both the US and Canada. The last page of the manual had the following notation. "The business of the De Laval Company is exclusively a cash one and all orders should be accompanied by remittance to cover; in the form of draft, check, postal or express money order or cash." There were obviously no large account receivable ledgers in the De Lava Company in the 1920's.

For years the Cream Separator was kept in the back porch of grandma's house. Its working days now long over it has assumed a new role as an attractive container for flowers in our back yard in St. Albert.

Remarkably grandma's bakers table with its heavy porcelain top and large pull out storage bins is still around. If I remember correctly grandma had it in the northeast corner of her kitchen. Why it did not get sold with the other furniture in their farm sale we will never know. Perhaps grandma was not willing to part with it. One wonders how many hundreds of loaves of bread, cookies, and other delicious baking items were prepared on its well-worn surface. Why this old piece of kitchen furniture survived is an interesting story.

In 1952 when dad and mom built their cabin at the lake they wisely decided that grandma's baking table would make an excellent addition to their kitchen furniture. For the next forty-six years it provided a very useful part of the many meals that were prepared at the lake. In 1998 when the cabin was torn down to make way for our new home most of the furniture was discarded. As I mentioned previously grandfather's old ornate easy chair was kept. I could not bring myself to discard grandma's baking table so it was stored in one of our small sheds at the lake. However eight years later when we sold our home at the lake I was again faced with the difficult decision on what to do with this old piece of furniture. Wisely it was kept and is now part of a section of our downstairs recreational room devoted to family keepsakes. Its sturdy surface is now a storage area for many other family keepsakes. One of which is grandma's kitchen wall mounted coffee bean grinder with its long handle. Also Fee we have mom's well worn light Aluminum bread mixing pan which she prepared the dough for those cinnamon buns which you thoroughly enjoyed many years back.

How grandma's armchair from her dining room table set survived is also an interesting story. In 1972 when dad and mom bought their modular home they had grandma's original dining room table chairs restored. To fit in their kitchen the table length was also reduced. When mom eventually moved to the Morinville Lodge she passed on to Tracy who had it for many years. After years in storage and many moves Tracy reluctantly parted with it. However I decided to keep grandma's armchair belonging to the dining room set. I have fond memories of grandma seated in her armchair at the far end of the dining room table during Sunday evening family meals at the farm. We now have it also on display in our downstairs recreation room.

Why the March 1948 copy of a farm magazine called the Country Gentleman was not discarded I have no idea. Perhaps the photo of the pastoral setting showing a flock of sheep on the cover reminded grandma of the days when they raised sheep on their Dakota farm.

The magazine was published at Independence Square, Philadelphia, Pennsylvania. It contained a lot of excellent reading for grandma to enjoy on a cold winter night. By today's standards this magazine was huge containing one hundred seventy pages each thirteen by ten inches in size. The subscription price was one dollar for two years. Its contents were equivalent to perhaps six issues of current monthly magazines.

It also had a very large section entitled the Country Women. With the amount of wear on the old pages they appear to have been very well read.

With grandma's love of farming she no doubt found most of the contents very interesting.

In looking over the many pages of advertising it is interesting how cigarette smoking was very much in vogue on the late 1940's. The first full page add inserted by a Tobacco Company featured a large photo of than Metropolitan Opera Star Rise Stevens holding a Chesterfield cigarette. Her glowing endorsement assures the reader that Chesterfield cigarettes were always milder, better tasting and cooler smoking. Not to be outdone by the Chesterfield add the Camel cigarette people also had a full page promoting their brand of cigarettes.

Unbelievable as it may sound some sixty plus years later they also featured a large photo of a then National League Hockey star Cal Gardiner. In his endorsement of Camel cigarettes he indicated that he had fifteen years playing experience with the New York Rangers.

It gets better at the bottom of the same page the following headline exclaimed." More Doctors smoke Camels than any other cigarette". To give more creditability to this assertion the following facts were in small print at the bottom. It stated that of 113,597 doctors surveyed more doctors smoked Camel than any other brand.

To give the above facts credence grandma Joyce indicated that in her early nursing career many doctors smoked cigarettes and cigars. This happened mostly while they were getting information on their patients while standing at the Nursing Station. Thankfully grandma has had no problems so far with all the second hand smoke she inhaled during her early nursing days.

CHAPTER NINETY-THREE

Cousin Ron McGillivray related the following story of grandma's experiment of using novel decorations on her Christmas tree many years ago. Prior to the arrival of electricity on the farm different ideas were used to brighten up the family tree at holiday time. One year, grandma decided as an addition to her customary tree decorations she would have real candles as an added attraction to her Christmas tree. Grandma's intentions of having burning candles on her tree did not go unnoticed by her two daughters living in the city. The real concern was the potential for real disaster should the whole tree become ignited in flames by the burning candle decorations. I am not exactly sure if grandma issued an invitation for the family to come out for Christmas or Aunt Margaret and Aunt Kathryn politely suggested their families would like to spend Christmas with grandma at the farm.

However it was agreed that Otterson and McGillivray families would spend Christmas day with grandma. Ron particularly remembers dad doing a lot of preparatory work in getting all grandma's gas lamps ready to brighten up the house interior prior to the evening Christmas meal. In a subtle way maybe dad was attempting to convince grandma she did not require the extra lighting that her tree candles would provide. Apparently grandma's candles were allowed to burn briefly for all the family to admire. However I have a feeling that all the adults present closely monitored the whole candle lighting procedure. Sadly I think this was grandma's last attempt to brighten up her Christmas tree using candlepower. It would be some years into the future before grandma would have the magic of electricity to assist her at Christmas time in safely lighting up her Christmas tree.

Thanks to cousin Fee's excellent memory he remembers a family Christmas gathering some years later at grandma's. According to Fee it was in 1938 two years before he entered the seminary. A family photo taken on grandma's front steps on that occasion is shown following.

at grandma Stevens' farm

**Left to Right; Ron, Grandma, Dad, Aunt Margaret, Myra, Fee,
Consuella, Uncle Mac
Front Row; Ann, Rita May, Gertrude**

The picturesque 1940 winter scene shown following would have been very representative of how grandma's home and yard appeared as the family arrived at the farm to spend their 1938 Christmas with grandma.

CHAPTER NINETY-FOUR

In the following chapter we will discuss some highlights of family and farm happenings in the 1940's. Our first story perhaps could be entitled the reluctant high school dance attendee.

The late spring photo of 1940 following has Fee and his sister Consuella wearing their Sunday best prior to attending his grade twelve graduation dance at the McDonald Hotel. If I recall correctly the photo is from Aunt Margaret's photo Album. In talking with Fee recently he mentioned his initial reluctance to attend the festivities at the McDonald. Apparently his objections were met with deaf ears by his parents. They were adamant in that Fee had an obligation to be present at his grade twelve graduation dance. However as reluctant as Fee was to attend his younger sister Consuella was quite looking forward to accompanying her older brother to the evening at the MacDonald Hotel. By the time the photo was taken I assume Fee was resigned to attending the graduation dance at the Mac. We note from the photo that Fee shows some facial expressions of enthusiasm to correspond to Consuela's look of anticipation for the evening that lies ahead of them.

1940 was a banner year on the Stevens farm in that the traditional prairie harvest scene of a threshing machine and crew was conspicuously absent. Instead dad had decided to try a new strange looking top-heavy machine called a combine to harvest his crop. It was one of the first combines to be used in our immediate area. Many of the neighbors did not consider it a step forward in harvesting technology. One of the better farmers in the area a French Canadian gentleman named Delphus Bourbonnais said to dad "John what are you doing throwing your grain on the ground?" He was of course referring to dad swathing his grain as opposed to doing it the traditional way with horses and a binder. In his mind the old way of harvesting grain was far superior.

Dad persevered using his combine and a few years later purchased a Massey Harris #21 self propel combine. Seventy years later a few dedicated individuals who wish to preserve the harvest threshing tradition for future generations run the only threshing machines operating on farms. Also some vintage threshing machines can be seen parked silently at the edges of farmers' fields along Alberta country roads. Their presence serves as a reminder of a proud bygone era of prairie agriculture.

The 1940 harvest photo of dad's new combine following was taken at the West place or the former Fritz farm. Although this somewhat tall awkward looking combine appears like a relic from the past at the time it represented the latest in harvesting technology. Their faithful John Deere D tractor is shown in front of the combine supplying the power to operate it. On the upper far right hand side of the photo is the home the Fritz family moved into when they came from South Dakota. Dad is now where to be seen in the picture however he was perhaps at the rear of the combine making some necessary adjustments to his new machine.

In July of 1941cousin Frank Collins came up to visit Grandma and the family. It had been seventeen years since the Stevens family stopped at the Collins farm on their return trip home to Alberta. Frank was now in the U.S. Merchants Marines and no doubt was on leave at the time.

While visiting Frank took some excellent family photos. My favorite is a photograph he took of grandma standing on the steps south of the house in front of the Sun Porch. Frank had it developed in color and sent it back to grandma when he returned home.

228

In the late 1943 summer photo following, the family had no doubt gathered at grandma's for a Sunday afternoon outing. Considering the time of year grandma's home raised spring broiler chickens would have been on the menu for supper that evening. Grandma was an excellent host and always served a delicious meal to her guests.

The one anomaly in the photo is the sports jacket yours truly is wearing. It had been purchased for my Confirmation that was earlier in the summer. Considering it was my first suit jacket I became quite attached to it. Mom in her wisdom perhaps realized that by the next summer the cuffs of the sleeves would be half way up to my elbows. She therefore must have relented to my requests and allowed me to wear it for the family gathering at grandma's. I perhaps wanted to emulate dad and my Uncles who always wore their Sunday best for our family Sunday afternoon gathering.

Family photo est. 1943

We are not certain when the Fritz family moved from Raton to Albuquerque, New Mexico. However Cousin Ann Littleton remembers her grandmother having a hair salon in the downstairs area of the Alvarado Hotel in Albuquerque. Having this fact I contacted the Albuquerque

Museum and was pleasantly surprised with the information they were able to locate.

The 1945 Albuquerque phone directory had a listing for the family under the heading Frank Fritz, Boiler Maker, A. T. and S. F. Railroad (Atchison, Topeka and Santa Fe). Their residence was listed as the Korber Apartments in Albuquerque. There was not a separate number for Aunt Irene's beauty salon however Alvarado Hotel Beauty and Barber Shop was listed in the 1945 directory. Having no idea of the Hotel's storied past I was pleasantly surprised when the Museum indicated that they had recently published an excellent history book about the Alvarado entitled Jewel of the Railroad Era.

In 1902 the Atchison Topeka and Santa Fe Railroad built a large elegant two story mission style hotel and railroad station in Albuquerque. It extended over a two-block area and was a focal point of the city for many years. Cousin Ann Littleton recalls staying there with her Arizona All State High School Band while they were performing in Albuquerque.

In 1946 the magic of electricity came to the Stevens farm however not from overhead power lines but courtesy of a gas Delco engine and batteries that dad had purchased. The many batteries that were used to store the electricity were kept in the old log shop. The gas engine that was required to generate the power for the batteries was also located in the shop. The Delco was started whenever the batteries indicated they needed charging. Perhaps my most vivid memory of having electric lights was the many exterior metal lines that carried the power to the lights. If I close my eyes I can still see the light brown metal exterior lines extending similar to spider webs to all the electrical outlets and lights in the house.

Shortly after we got electricity dad built an overhead water line from the pump house to grandma's attic. A large new galvanized tank was installed in the attic with gravity allowing the water to be piped to her kitchen and bathroom. A hot water jacket was installed in her cook stove which allowed her to have hot water at all times. Although grandma was now in the twilight years of her life I am sure she thoroughly enjoyed her new modern conveniences.

231

There was another innovation in grandma house although I am not sure what year it was installed or how happy grandma was with it. It was the brown metal oil-burning heater located in the center of her living room. Grandma's originally had an attractive black ornate wood and coal heater with silver trim in the area now occupied by the oil heater. With the new oil stove grandma was totally dependent on dad to keep it operating relinquishing some of her prized spirit of independence. Also I don't think grandma was totally convinced of her new stoves reliability on cold winter nights.

In 1948 grandma would also have the pleasure of attending three of her older grandchildren's celebrations as they embarked on their chosen career paths in life. It was also a memorable year for the family in that May 29th marked grandma's eightieth birthday.

The first special celebration of the year was her grandson Fee's ordination at St. Joseph's Cathedral in Edmonton on February 8th 1948. The extreme cold winter weather that accompanied your Ordination Fee helped immeasurably in my ability to recall events of your special day. An original copy of the invitation to Fee's Ordination taken from mom's keepsakes is shown below.

The Reverend Felix Ottarson

cordially invites you to be present at his

Ordination to the Holy Priesthood

to be conferred by

The Most Reverend

John Hugh MacDonald, D.D.

Archbishop of Edmonton

Sunday morning, the Eighth of February

nineteen hundred and forty-eight

at seven-thirty o'clock in

St. Joseph's Cathedral

and to offer with him his

First Solemn Mass

Sunday morning, the Fifteenth of February

at eleven o'clock in

St. Joseph's Cathedral

Edmonton, Alberta

Reception: 10227 - 115 St.
2:30 - 5:30 P.M.
Sunday, February 8th

As we discussed earlier in recalling our family history road and weather conditions could present a challenge when planning a trip away from the farm. This was the case when my parents made travel plans to attend Fee's Ordination. Not trusting the elements they made the wise decision that the family including grandma should spend the night prior to Fee's ordination in the city. To a twelve-year-old country kid this sounded like an exciting overnight adventure. Grandma I think stayed at Aunt Margaret's and we stayed at that venerable old city landmark the Selkirk Hotel on the corner of Jasper and 101st.

In speaking with Fee recently he could not give me a definite reason why the Ordination service was scheduled so early Sunday morning. This of course required what I perceived as us getting up very early in strange surroundings to attend the 7.30 A. M. service. I don't recall much about the drive to the

Cathedral however I wondered why there was no large imposing church in sight when we arrived at the Cathedral. Instead there was this large rambling one story stucco building with many huge brown wooden doors facing the street. I was again surprised when we went inside and immediately went down into a spacious lower level of what I apparently described to mom as an underground church.

Fee said Archbishop McDonald ordained three priests that Sunday morning Ed McCarty, Mike McNally and himself. Interestingly Ed McCarty who was from a large farm at Big Valley, Alberta also had a degree in Agriculture from the University of Alberta.

February eight also marked the sixty-second birthday of Uncle Eddie Otterson making Fee's Ordination day very special for him. As the invitation indicated there was an open house at the Otterson home from two to five on the afternoon of the Ordination. In talking to Gertrude recently she indicated they had arranged to have an easy chair for grandma upstairs where all the gifts Fee had received were displayed. My only memory of the afternoon reception at the Otterson home was Aunt Margaret's insistence that the younger members of the family help themselves to many trays of treats available to the guests.

McGillivray - Biollo May Wedding
Four months later on May 27th grandma's grandson Ronald McGillivray married Frances Biollo at St. Anthony's pro Cathedral in Edmonton. Ron's newly ordained cousin Fee officiated at Ron and Fran's wedding.

Mr. and Mrs. Peter Paul Biollo

request the honour of your presence
at the marriage of their daughter

Frances Louise

to

Ronald Stevens McGillivray

on the morning of
Thursday, the twenty-seventh of May
nineteen hundred and forty-eight
at ten-thirty o'clock
St. Anthony's Pro-Cathedral
Edmonton, Alberta

Reception following ceremony
Corona Hotel

R.S.V.P.

Of special significance to grandma was all her children were able to be present at Ron and Fran's marriage celebration. The family is shown following all decked out in their wedding finery. I particularly was impressed with all the elegant hats the ladies were wearing.

235

Aunt Kathryn, Aunt Mae, Dad, Aunt Margaret, Grandma, Aunt Irene, Aunt Ellen

Although the younger cousins did not attend Ron's wedding I have a special memory of that beautiful spring morning of Ron and Fran's wedding. Cousin Kenneth McGillis and I were allowed to accompany our parents to the city. The highlight of our day was going for lunch on our own to the American Dairy Lunch. It was located downstairs on the south side of Jasper Avenue at one hundred and second street. I particularly remember the many different fancy dessert selections on display that for two hungry boys looked very enticing.

Ross – Otterson Wedding
The last family wedding of 1948 was grandma's granddaughter Consuella Otterson's marriage to Walter Ross on November 27th at the Cathedral with her brother Fee again officiating. A light reception was held later at the McDonald Hotel. According to Fee one the highlights of the reception was

236

the frequent exiting of many men from the banquet hall to check on the progress of a certain national sports event underway that day.

Their wedding day had coincided with that famous Grey Cup football game between the Calgary Stampeders and the Toronto Argonauts in Toronto where Calgary was victorious in bringing the Grey Cup back west.
Calgary also initiated in 1948 the pre game festivities that are now an important part of the Grey Cup Game. The Western Canadian hospitality extended to Torontonians by the Calgary contingent atop their horses and dressed in western attire set the stage for present pre Grey Cup game extravaganzas we all enjoy.

After their marriage Wally and Consuella lived in a small home which was a second residence located several blocks west of the Otterson home. The design of their home resembled a smaller version of grandma's chicken house on the farm that as far as grandma was concerned was nothing to be ashamed off.

On Sunday May 29th 1949 the family gathered at grandma's home to celebrate her eighty first birthday. No doubt because of Ron and Fran's wedding being held on May 27th the previous year there was no official family get together on her eightieth birthday. However in 1949 grandma's birthday coincided with Sunday the normal day of the week when the family got together at the farm in the summer months. I guess we could describe it as her belated eightieth birthday celebration. Besides the many grandchildren in attendance grandma had the honor of having some of her great grandchildren present. I don't recall too many highlights of the day. However thankfully many photos were taken which for many of us can help bring back the memory of grandma's special day.

Back Row; Wally, Consuella, Aunt Ellen, Nina, Aunt Mae, Aunt
Margaret, Dad, Fran, Aunt Kathryn
Second Row; Gertrude, Ron, Grandma, Fee, Uncle Mac
Front row, John Kirwin, Micheal Kirwin, Myself, Myra, Anna, Donna
Anne, Rita Mae

Ron, Dad, Grandma, Fee

Back Row; Aunt Ellen, Dad. Aunt Margaret,
Front Row; Aunt Mae, Grandma, Kathryn

Four generations; Aunt Mae, Grandma, Nina , John Kirwin

CHAPTER NINETY-FIVE

On November 16th 1951 at eighty-three years of age grandma passed away peacefully at the General Hospital in Edmonton. Grandma had been a guest at the McGillivray home in the city where unfortunately she had a fall and broke her hip. She was admitted to the General Hospital where she subsequently developed pneumonia and passed away. During last days in the hospital grandma told Cousin Gertrude Bohan that she was looking for forward to joining John (grandfather) in the next world.

Grandma's prayers or what was then commonly referred to as a wake were held the following Sunday evening at her home on the farm. Her grandson Father Fee Otterson said the funeral Mass the following Monday morning at St. Emmerence church in Riviere Qui Barre. Grandma was laid to rest beside grandfather in St. Joachim's cemetery in Edmonton with their headstone shown following.

In looking at grandma's well-lived life I think a summary of some of the highlights of her life should be reviewed. The hardships faced by the young Franz family while living in Iowa although not unique for members of grandma's generation no doubt were valuable character building experiences. These early lessons of the hardships of life were later reinforced when grandma and her siblings helped their ailing parents in operating the family business at Woonsocket, South Dakota. Their subsequent move to their farm when grandma was seventeen no doubt opened up a whole new world of hard physical labor to her.

As fate would have it grandfather was living on a neighboring farm close to the Franz family farm. This eventually resulted in the beginning of a serious relationship between the two young farm neighbors. Their courting days were not without challenges chiefly due to her father's reluctance to bestow his blessing on his daughter's proposed marriage to grandfather. Ironically grandfather's approval rating must have improved dramatically because several years later great grandfather Franz sold the farm to my grandparents.

Aunt Mae's description of her early childhood days on their Dakota farm speaks volumes of the happy times grandma and the family enjoyed while living there. After living on their Dakota farm for twenty-three years the family made the decision to begin a new life in Alberta.

Grandma's remaining thirty-seven years in Alberta had their share of adversity with grandfather's passing after only living in Alberta for eleven years. However with the family getting larger grandma became very involved in the lives of her family. I think some of grandma's most enjoyable years where when the grandchildren stayed with her during their summer holidays at the farm.

As I previously mentioned grandma had some very strong character traits. She always seemed to be in charge whatever the circumstances. Grandma's mottos in life were actions always speak much louder than words. Grandma never lost her pride in her former South Dakota roots to the point that she never could force herself to become a Canadian citizen. Grandma had a fierce pride in her family and their accomplishments. She also took great pride in the tasks at hand whether it be gardening, raising chickens or baking cookies in her kitchen. In summary I think we can all remember grandma as our family's own Iron Lady.

CHAPTER NINETY-SIX

Although the family history concluded in 1951 with grandma's passing I think I would be remiss not to recognize the recent passing of three long-lived family members. Remarkably together they achieved a total of three hundred plus years of productive living.

The first one of the three to pass on was cousin Frank Collins a son of grandma's youngest sister Alice.

Frank was born on April 14th 1906 at Canistota, South Dakota to Harry and Alice Collins. Frank always maintained that he was born on April 14th and also came into the world weighing fourteen pounds.

Frank had two older sisters Edith and Florence who both remained in the Canistota area their entire lives. After finishing his schooling and working for a while, Frank enlisted in the United States Merchant Marines or Sea Bee's as he referred to his Navy service unit.

Frank who was a confirmed bachelor had the opportunity to travel to many exotic tropical destinations during his many years of service with the Marines. He soon realized there were more pleasant places to live particularly in the cold winter months than his former South Dakota home.

He wisely decided upon retirement to put roots down in Honolulu buying a one-bedroom condo there. Frank however he did not want to totally abandon his Dakota roots so for many years he spent the winters in Hawaii and the summers back in the States.

After an absence of forty years Frank returned to visit his Alberta cousins in 1981. In the photo following he is shown standing by his van while on his Alberta visit. When not staying with friends of relatives the van served as Frank's home away from home. At the time of the photo Frank was seventy-five years old. He would continue to spend his summers in the States visiting relatives and friends well up into his eighties.

The letter following was sent to mom by Frank when he had safely arrived back in the U.S. after his 1981 summer visit to Alberta. By the content of the letter we can appreciate that Frank was well traveled during the summer months that he spent in the U. S.

Canistota, So. Dak.
Sept. 24 - 19 81

Dear Cousin,
I arrived here on
Sept. 15th and it seems that I
am always busy accomplishing
nothing. At least I am getting
a few letter written.

When I left Moinville
I went thru Saskatoon where
I stayed in a beautiful Camp
ground in town - $5.50 per nite.
On down thru Regina where
it was a pleasure and easy
to drive - no traffic circles
and good, well located street
signs. the Edmonton traffic
people should go to Regina
for some study courses.

then down to Minot
and east to Grand Forks. I had
no idea that there are so many
trees along there and it is so
pretty. they grow a lot of
sun flowers there now,

247

7 From Grand Forks down the west side of the river thru the fertile Red River Valley to Fargo; then east to Saint Paul, Minn.

Mabel, Viola and Marcella were at Sister Jessie's. And I met more cousins I hadn't known about. I stayed with Tom (Sister's oldest son) and Tim (the youngest) at Tom's place. They took me around to see the sights.

I visited friends in Minneapolis who also took me around. I drove up to Pine River — 175 miles — to visit a friend who grew up here. The last time I saw him was in 1934. It was a good visit and I am pleased that I made the trip.

When I arrived here it was chilly — a cold north wind had come up. Since then it has been beautiful weather

248

3)

most of the time. One of
these days it will be sudden
winter as so often happens.

Edith is busy with the
house, garden etc. and today
is canning tomatoes. Florence is
getting along very well at the
nursing home. She gets out
and walks a good deal. A few
days ago I took her to Sioux
Falls shopping. She found out
she can't do as much as she
thinks she can.

I will leave here Oct. 6th or 7th
for Phoenix, Arizona. From there
I may go to Tucson on my
way to San Diego, then Long
Beach and Boulder City on the
way to Reno. Then get ready
to go to Hawaii Nov. 18th. I will
be glad to be there again.

Naa I really enjoyed my
visit to Canada and the time
spent with you and Ellen and

the rest. It was wonderful
of you and Ellen to take
me around so much to
see so many things. Again
I thank you for all of
you hospitality.
　　　And please extend my
greetings to Jack and family.

　　　　　　　Sincerely,

　　　　　　　　　Frank.

Maybe you will get
over to Hawaii again this
winter — or next,
　　　　　　　F,

Remarkably Frank lived on his own in his condo until December of 2008 when he moved into an assisted living facility in Honolulu. Cousin Fee Otterson had the opportunity to visit him while he was in the assisted living facility. Fee said they had a good visit particularly about when my grandparents lived on their farm in South Dakota.

Frank passed away peacefully last year in July in the assisted living facility at one hundred and three years young. He had long ago selected a plot in the

Canistota cemetery located just east of town on land donated by his grandfather Herman Collins.

Approximately six months later on January 8th 2010 Frank's first cousin Ellen McGillis also one hundred and three years young passed away peacefully at the Dickensfield Long Term Care facility in Edmonton, Alberta. For years the two had exchanged phone calls and cards on their respective birthdays.

Following is a short summary of Aunt Ellen's well-lived life that she wrote on the occasion of her hundred birthday celebration.

Ellen McGillis - My History

Written by Ellen to celebrate her 100th birthday

I was born on December 18, 1906 on a farm near Canistota, South Dakota, the youngest of six and the fifth daughter of John and Mary Stevens. In 1914 we came to Alberta arriving at Morinville on March 7th. Our farm was located one mile east and three miles north of Riviere Que Barre. We went to school at Belle Valley and finished our high school in Morinville.

In 1926 I went to McTavish Business College in Edmonton taking a secretarial course. Angus McGillis came on the scene taking me back to Edmonton on the weekends. He had a new 1926 Chevy Sedan, which was something in those days. At that time our beaus came for Sunday night supper, thinking they might be getting a good cook. Mother did most of the cooking.

On November 5, 1929 we were married at St. Emerence Church in Riviere Que Barre. Our home was two miles east and three miles south of R.Q.B. where I lived until 1995. The Great Depression had started in October, being in love it didn't register for months.

In the fall a grain tank of oats sold for $8.00, which was the price of a barrel of tractor fuel. Tractors were not used for field work, only for threshing in those times.

In August of 1935 Angus went to a political meeting at Glengary School, it was the beginning of the Social Credit era. When he came home he said there was a frost, I asked "how much?" he said "I'll go to the garden and see." He brought in a couple of frozen pea vines, pulled the covers back on the bed and put them in with me. I didn't doubt him. This occurred on the first night of the full moon in August. I have been wary of it ever since.

On November 21, 1936 our son, Kenneth was born. That same year there was a drought. We did mixed farming which meant we had horses, cattle, pigs, chickens and turkeys. The turkeys were for the Christmas market for the housewife's Christmas money. I think most of the butcher shop merchants saw us farm women coming, the Christmas gifts weren't too lavish.

On August 27, 1944 we welcomed our daughter Marion into our family, that year we had a good crop.

In November 1949 we got our first telephone and the Calgary Power came on in the same month. Oh! life was good, no more lamps and lanterns to fill and chimneys to wash. Gas lamps to fill with "High Test Gas" and be careful of the mantles.

In November 1952 we bought our first 'new car', a Chevy Sedan from one of the Borle boys who was an agent in our neighborhood. We had cars most of the time which are now classed as 'previously owned', some I think several times. This was such a great event in our lives; we took a trip to Vermillion where Kenneth was going to Agriculture School. We landed there on "Sadie Hawkins" day; he wasn't able to spend the evening with us because he had a girl taking him to the show. By the time of the Christmas holidays, he was 16 and could drive the car without Dad. He spent two winters at Vermillion, graduating in 1954.

On June 13, 1959 Kenneth and Irene McCambly were married in St. Patricks Church in Lethbridge. They lived in Edmonton until 1972.

In August 1965 Marion received her Registered Nursing Diploma from the Misericordia Hospital and married Allan Skakun on October 16 at St. Pius X Church in Edmonton.

In November of 1968 natural gas was turned on and now things couldn't really be any better. No more coal buckets and oil for the heater.

In 1972 Kenneth, Irene and their three children, Larry, Leslie and Kelly built a home near us on the farm which made Angus and myself very happy. On October 27, 1973 Angus died of cancer. Becoming a widow took a bit of adjusting, but life goes on.

In the meantime, Marion and Al had given us four more grandchildren, Karen, Mark, Dale and Tracy. They lived in Edmonton, and then moved to Sherwood Park and from there to St. Albert in April 1977 where they bought a home.

Some of my friends had become widows, some before me, some after. The McDonell sisters were in the category. Margaret Armstrong, Ruth Ouimet and Ethel Graf. They had taken many trips. I joined the group. We went from California to Inuvik, Vancouver to Prince Edward Island and four weeks in the British Isles.

In the summer of 1982 I purchased a two bedroom trailer. My families, with the help of Jack, Kenny, Gerard and Allan McRae, demolished the old house and set up the trailer. So now I had a new home.

In 1985 Jack McRae became 65 years old and decided to quit farming. He had rented our land for 20 years so Kenneth and Irene are the farmers now.

In January 1988 my daughter Marion died of cancer and nine months later, her son Dale was killed in a motorcycle accident. It was not a good year.

In 2000 I stopped driving. I was 94 years old and knew that on my 95th birthday I had to have a medical certificate from the doctor to continue driving. I enjoyed my drives to Morinville however I didn't want to push my luck. By 2003 I was finding making my own meals a little tedious and decided to move to Heritage Lodge in Morinville, I was 96 years old.

I lived there from January 15, 2003 to July 4, 2004. I enjoyed my time there and made many friends. In July of 2004 I had a spell of not feeling so well and I decided to move to Dickensfield where the folks would keep a close eye on me. I have the blessing of many visitors, both family and friends. I still enjoy watching Curling and Baseball and of course Jeopardy on TV. I enjoy my glass of Sherry every day following lunch. I have gone out on a few of the 'trips' with the group at Dickensfield and still enjoy family dinners with the gang on occasion.

I have lived a very blessed life with my 6 grandchildren and 14 great grandchildren and many special friends and family members.

So this is my life, 100 years! I have been happy with it!

253

As an added note perhaps one of the reasons that contributed to Aunt Ellen's long well lived life was her daily routine of enjoying a glass of Sherry. She also never failed to offer her many visitors to share a glass of Sherry with her. Her standard line was would you like a glass of wine? There are some clean glasses over on the table help yourself. If the bottle of Sherry in her room happened to be on the low side there always seemed to be a full replacement bottle in her closet.

Eleven days after Aunt Ellen passing our cousin Vera Miller passed away peacefully at ninety seven years of age at the Ironwood Health and Rehab center at South Bend, Indiana. Vera was the oldest of my grandparent's sixteen grandchildren and had accompanied her family when they came to Alberta from South Dakoa.

Following is a short summary of Vera's well-lived life sent to us recently by her daughter Ann Littleton.

Dear All - Mother died this morning. She had been in Hospice care for a week. I think she was the most peaceful that she has ever been for this week. It has been a long year but she is now at peace. This obit will be in the South Bend paper, the Santa Fe paper, and the San Antonio paper. Ann

Vera Littleton Miller

August 23, 1912 - January 19, 2010

Vera Miller, 97, passed away at Ironwood Health and Rehab.

Vera was born in Parker, South Dakota, in 1912. Her parents were Frank Joseph Fritz (1887-1960) and Vera Irene Stevens (1890-1978). About 1913 her family moved to Alberta, Canada. Because of her mother's poor health, they were told to move to New Mexico. In 1915, they moved to Raton, New Mexico, where Vera and her brother Leonard grew up. After graduation from Raton High School, she attended beauty college in Denver and started working as a beautician.

In 1937 she moved to Santa Fe, New Mexico, where she met and married Glen Berlin Littleton (1912-1975). They had three children, one of whom lived only six hours.

After Glen's death, she took a trip to the Holy Land where she met Oscar Edwin Miller (1897-1989) of San Antonio. They were married in 1978 and she moved to San Antonio, Texas.

In 2002 she moved to South Bend, Indiana, to be nearer her daughter.

Vera was a beautician for over 50 years. She was a member of the United Methodist Church in Santa Fe and later in San Antonio. She was an amateur artist and won three awards from a senior citizen art contest in Texas. She loved to grow flowers and had a large flower garden in Santa Fe.

Vera is survived by two children: Richard (Judi) Littleton who lives in Austin, Texas, and Ann Littleton, who lives in South Bend. She has two grandchildren and four great-grandchildren. Her ashes will be interred at the National Cemetery in Santa Fe. There will be a memorial service for the family in June.

Contributions in Vera's memory may be made to Fairview Cemetery Preservation Association, PO Box 5958, Santa Fe, New Mexico 87502.

19/01/2010

In November of 2002 Vera sent me a beautiful colored wall mural painting that was a treasured keepsake of hers. The painting featured great grandfather John Stevens seated in his Rochester Art studio. She made the following comment on the back of the painting. "I am giving this to Jack Stevens. I hope you enjoy it as much as I have." We now have it displayed on the wall in our recreation room with other early family photos.

Vera Miller 94 years young; 2006

We also have a copy of a paintings Vera did from an old family photo taken immediately south of my grandparents home on the farm. In the painting grandma is standing beside their Overland car with grandfather and some family members seated in the car.

In 2006 Vera's daughter Ann sent following column shown following on how art can help us remember special things that are no longer part of our lives. Sharon Dettmer of the Tribune with the headline wrote it. Her art prompts memories.

Her art prompts memories

■ Vera Miller, 93, recalls when she lived, worked in Southwest.

By SHARON DETTMER
Tribune Correspondent

SOUTH BEND

Memories fade.
That's why Vera Miller, 93, surrounds herself with paintings and pictures to preserve those memories. Art that she created during her mid-life serves as a constant visual reminder of living in the Southwest.

Those memories are refreshing.

Her walls are covered with paintings, drawings, counted-cross-stitch creations and embroidery, reflecting days spent in Santa Fe, N.M., or in Red River, N.M. That's where

Vera Miller recreated a painting of an African mother and child that she had seen in a magazine. Miller was attracted to the rich skin tones of the subjects in this portrait, she said.

she often fished, sketched, or hiked and viewed breathtaking scenery with family.

Miller lived in Santa Fe from 1930 to 1978.

She then resided in San Antonio after retiring as a beautician.

See MEMORIES/E2

FROM PAGE E1

Memories

In 2002 Miller moved to South Bend in order to spend time with her daughter, Ann Littleton. Littleton retired from teaching music for the School City of Mishawaka. She enjoys viewing her mother's art, and reminiscing.

Miller lives at St. Paul's Retirement Community.

Two of the artist's paintings are on display in Chapel Lane at St. Paul's, along with the works of other residents.

Her artistic endeavor was born of a gift.

"When I die and go to heaven," she always told her first husband, Glen Littleton, "I'll learn how to paint."

Glen, now deceased, wanted his wife to cultivate artistic talents while living in this world. So, on her 59th birthday, he purchased art brushes and watercolors for her.

And Glen also provided a private space for her to create.

Paint, she did.

Miller received formal art training in the 1960s at College of Santa Fe, a liberal arts school.

Immersing herself in art, she learned techniques quickly, and even studied with a local artist.

Watercolors, oil paintings, acrylics, Chinese, Native American and African-themed art, and pen-and-ink drawings depicting her South Dakota childhood were created.

Some are award-winning works of art.

Miller was a multi-finalist and second-place winner of "Art is Ageless" contests while in San Antonio. The annual art contests are sponsored by Texas Association of Homes and Services for the Aging and Educational Institute on Aging.

She has the heart of an artist.

"I always think, 'Tomorrow, I might go outside and sketch,'" Miller said, with a faint smile.

These days, physical challenges prohibit her from doing so. Still, her artistic powers of observation are very keen.

"I've learned to be observant. I can look at a tree to really see the true texture of the bark," she explained. Observation is essential, in both art and in life, she added. "Whether you ever paint a picture or not, being observant is still a great skill to have."

I particularly like the last paragraph and the last sentence in which she said. "Whether you ever paint a picture or not, being observant is still a great skill to have."

Jack and Joyce Stevens, 2010

9 780980 953497